Poverty, Power, and Authority in Education

CROSS-CULTURAL PERSPECTIVES

Edited by
EDGAR B. GUMBERT
Georgia State University

Center for Cross-cultural Education
College of Education
Georgia State University
Atlanta, Georgia

Library of Congress Cataloging in Publication Data

Main entry under title:

Poverty, power, and authority in education.

Edited papers originally presented as lectures at Georgia State University, April-May, 1981 in the visiting scholar lecture series.

Includes bibliographical references.
Contents: Education against poverty: interpreting British and American policies in the 1960s and 1970s / Harold Silver—Ideology and educational research / Michael F.D. Young—Deference to authority, education in Canada and the United States / Edgar Z. Friedenberg.
 1. Education and state—Addresses, essays, lectures.
 2. Educational research—Addresses, essays, lectures.
 I. Gumbert, Edgar B., 1931-   II. Silver, Harold. Education against poverty. 1981.   III. Young, Michael F. D., Ideology and educational research, 1981.
 IV. Friedenberg, Edgar Zodiag, 1921-   Deference to authority, education in Canada and the United States. 1981.

LC87.P68   370'.7'8   81-7140

ISBN 0-88406-149-3   AACR2

Preparation and design by:
Business Publishing Division
College of Business Administration
Georgia State University
University Plaza
Atlanta, Georgia 30303
Telephone: 404-658-4253

Copyright © 1981 by Center for Cross-cultural Education

All rights reserved, including the right to reproduce the publication, or portions therof, in any form without prior permission from the publisher.

Georgia State University is an equal educational opportunity institution and an equal opportunity/ affirmative action employer.

Georgia State University is a unit of the University System of Georgia.

Printed in the United States of America.

Contents

Introduction
Edgar B. Gumbert   1

Education Against Poverty: Interpreting British and American Policies in the 1960s and 1970s
Harold Silver   13

Ideology and Educational Research
Michael F.D. Young   35

Deference to Authority: Education in Canada and the United States
Edgar Z. Friedenberg   45

EDGAR B. GUMBERT is Professor of Educational Foundations at Georgia State University. He established the Center for Crosscultural Education in the College of Education in 1980. He is the author of *The Superschool and The Superstate: American Education in the Twentieth Century, 1918-1970* and of articles and essays in a variety of journals and periodicals.

Introduction
Edgar B. Gumbert

The papers included in this volume were originally presented as lectures at Georgia State University in April and May, 1981. They were the first set of lectures given in the Visiting Scholar Lecture Series sponsored annually by the Center for Cross-Cultural Education and the College of Education, and they have been only slightly revised for publication.

The speakers were not asked to conform to a single theme for the lecture series; rather, they were invited to prepare lectures based on research currently in progress or recently completed.

There is considerable coherence among the issues investigated and the concerns expressed in the papers, and this is a result of their common ties to a recent period of educational history—the 1960s and 1970s. Harold Silver has set himself the formidable task of writing an educational history of the 1960s and 1970s, with special attention to the effects of education on poverty. Both of the other speakers in the series made singular contributions to the intellectual life of those decades. Michael F.D. Young placed the sociology of education and the sociology of knowledge at the center of debates about school policy. Edgar Z. Friedenberg called attention to such important educational matters as internal school organization, the methods of teaching and of evaluation employed in schools, and the varied and potent educational mechanisms by which dominant groups impose their educational and cultural ideas on subordinate groups.

Educators generally concede that the 1960s and 1970s constitute an especially important period in educational history. They also acknowledge that, despite the scholarly attention the period rightly has been given, its educational record still remains an enigma. No doubt the mystery arises in part from the difficulties inherent in writing an account of the recent past. It is hoped that the three studies included in this volume will to some extent overcome this problem and help to solve some of the several remaining mysteries of the 1960s and 1970s. The challenge is to see what worked for educators during this period, what didn't, and why.

The task of analyzing educational policies during the 1960s and 1970s is made easier by the existence during this period of significant similarities in the ideologies and institutions of industrial nations. This shared context framed the education problems and influenced the policies that were adopted for their solution. Especially in Britain and the United States there was substantial agreement on a broad range of social, political, and economic ideas and policies within which educational debates proceeded. There were at least two main points of convergence: First, government involvement in the management of the economy helped to coordinate the efforts and aims of capital and labor and attempted to minimize unemployment and inflation through a variety of educational and economic policies. Second, governments sought to provide a minimum standard of living below which none of their citizens could fall. This meant that governments provided services such as job training, health care, and moderate-cost housing that were not readily available from the private sector. Governments also provided features such as job safety, unemployment insurance, and environmental protection to help protect individuals from circumstances with which they could not contend alone.

In Britain these measures were thought of as elements of socialism; in the United States they were thought of as the politics of liberalism. Agreement was derived from common efforts to deal with similarly changing social realities. Both nations contended domestically with affluence and with rising economic and educational expectations. The broadly similar trends during this period encouraged educational and cultural borrowing. Educational ideas and practices were readily exchanged between Britain and the United States, as the paper by Harold Silver clearly shows. The educational war against poverty went from the United States to Britain, but the high hopes and the resourceful practices of "open education" travelled the other direction, to cite only two examples.

American liberalism, the ideological source for many of the educational ideas and practices that were transported to Britain throughout the 1960s and 1970s, was informed by several striking articles of faith, foremost among which was a devout belief in social justice, in the perfectablility of man and his world, and in a good life without limits for all. Liberal proponents of change saw themselves as messengers with a mandate to convert people to goodness both at home and abroad. The domestic and the foreign ideological fevers were connected and they burned simultaneously. They were derived from the optimistic conviction that the world could and should be made over. The liberal vision sought both to alleviate the inequities and inadequacies of the present age and to gratify emerging new expectations. At home liberals believed that the nation could be housed and fed, that deteriorating cities could be renovated, that alienation and misery could be eliminated. Abroad they tried to defeat communism by using military force and to build new nations by providing foreign loans and technical assistance. Policies in Vietnam disingenuously combined war and nation-building.

The decade of the 1960s especially was a period during which liberal ideology and the social sciences joined forces, united in their delight with the prospects of human and social engineering. Educationists promised remarkable solutions to individual and social problems made possible by an unprecedented application of new pedagogical materials and techniques. Their promises were consistent with the optimistic ideals of the time. It was believed that education, properly managed, could bring untold benefits to individuals and to society. Learning, technology, and human nature were linked. Human nature, it was claimed, could be changed by appropriate learning environments. New concepts and techniques of learning proliferated. The use of schooling as a social panacea was reflected in an emphasis on urban education, compensatory education, education for the disadvantaged or the "culturally deprived," Head Start, Upward Bound, and other related programs. Education strategies were put on and taken off like fashions. Parental opposition to them was considered a product of ignorance and an enemy to be fought and eliminated. All of the strategies promised to free people from the fetters that prevented them from reaching their full human potential.

The success of these foreign and domestic liberal programs rested on three foundations: on the truth of the various theories informing the policies that were being pursued; on the ability to pay for the policies; and on the general acceptance and perpetuation of established authorities—Congress, the President, political parties, schools and universities, among others.

Paradoxically, these foundations were being challenged at the very time the policies that rested on them were being most ardently applied. The theories were seen by critics to be integral parts of a messianic ideology that had a blinkered and narrow vision of what had to be done and of how to do it, both at home and abroad. According to the critics, selected aspects of American culture had been idealized, and any person who did not conform to them was thought to be either inferior or wicked, or both. Critics said that thoughtless pride and hatred rather than truth and fairness guided the ambitions of policy-makers.

It does seem now that the liberal ideology was at once vain and innocent. Things were promised that could not be delivered. Schooling alone could not heal the ills of American society, nor could military or political and economic intervention abroad create a brave new world.

Many expensive programs were based on hastily formulated and carelessly examined theories. This was perhaps especially true in education, where sensationalism and opportunism in research centers were at times in league with the wrongheadedness of some of its practitioners. When many of the liberal initiatives of the 1960s failed, or were perceived to have failed, attention turned quickly to their costs. Critics argued that expenditures on education and welfare services, and to a less extent on military services, involved no careful judgment on need or costs. Liberal programs, it was said, threw money at problems, and generally more was believed to be better. Educators frequently took this position. During the 1970s the incontrovertible discovery was made that America did not have the unlimited resources that would make possible endless casual experimentation and waste; there were material and social limits to national growth. The value of the dollar declined, the costs of vital imports increased, and the American position in the international economy weakened. The working assumption that more was better became intellectually and politically discredited by 1980.

The general acceptance of established authorities waned, partly as a consequence of their own policies and conduct. In one important sense the social reforms of the Great Society were aborted by their champions when they tried to bring their concept of a social democracy into existence by employing technocratic means. The protest movements of the 1960s reflected a general awareness that the major institutions and processes of American politics were in conflict with certain basic ideas about freedom, equality, and participatory forms of government. The feeling was that technocracy had replaced democracy. National affairs were managed from the top and were impervious to popular feeling. In the interests of "rationality" and "efficiency," Americans were governed according to what was deemed good for them. Congress, critics said, adapted itself to technocracy and transferred much of its power to nonelected experts.

Introduction / 5

Schools and universities, like Congress, lost some of their authority by allying themselves with technocratic elites, both public and private, and by assenting to discredited national military and industrial manpower objectives. Political parties, according to the critics, merely helped rationalize and legitimize an increasingly antidemocratic political system. The office of the President lost much of its authority as a result of President Nixon's unlawful conduct during his terms in office.

Similar criticisms of educational and political institutions were expressed in Britain during the 1960s and 1970s but the authority of British institutions was not as deeply challenged as it was in the United States. Nevertheless, the urban riots in Britain during the spring and summer of 1981 led some British leaders to liken the seriousness and difficulty of the challenge to the one faced by the United States in the 1960s. The riots in Britain raised questions familiar to Americans about problems of law enforcement, police-community relations, racial tensions, youth unemployment, urban decay, rising crime, and political extremism.

Similarities should not be stressed too much, of course, but the debate in Britain in 1981 produced arguments about causes and cures for these problems similar to those of the Kerner Commission, appointed by President Johnson to investigate riots in the United States in the 1960s. Major programs to fight poverty and improve race relations were called for. The scale of the riots to date has been comparatively smaller than the riots in the United States during the 1960s; but the challenge to established authorities may prove to be a historical watershed similar to the one produced by the riots and the civil rights movement in the United States in that decade.

Today we are experiencing a moment of more than routine interest in educational history. In virtually all nations, especially industrial nations, new answers to educational questions and new approaches are being sought in efforts to legitimize (or to relegitimize) the authority of schools and of school knowledge. In order to understand the potential of an educational system's present, it is necessary to understand its past.

The historical work to reevaluate the educational record in Britain and the United States in the 1960s and 1970s has now begun, as the paper by Harold Silver included in this volume attests. Important questions are being asked. Issues relate to success and failure and to a selection from among the many educational initiatives of those decades of the projects that should be continued, even if in modified form.

In the United States today there is a strong and persistent feeling that the educational hopes of the 1960s and 1970s were grand—and failed—illusions. Accomplishments regularly fell short of intentions. Inadequacies and imperfections in educational theory and practice during those decades now loom very large.

Perhaps it is not surprising that an exaggerated assessment of what could be done was followed by an equally exaggerated assessment of failure. The fervent educational efforts in the 1960s and 1970s were instigated by ideology, and it is likely that the reactions to those efforts also have a strong ideological component.

Scholars like Harold Silver who are especially interested in the 1960s and 1970s are only beginning to be able to evaluate aims against results. Of course, it is entirely possible that educational programs in those decades included more subtle and more various work than has been commonly thought by critics. Failure in all educational efforts is not obvious nor has it been conclusively demonstrated. It is also possible that some important and promising changes took place in perception and practice during those decades, and these changes should be properly evaluated in terms of context and of the continuity of the past with the present and the future. Schooling, as a result, might evolve into something with greater range and considerateness than it has displayed to date.

This important and puzzling period in educational history can probably best be understood by seeing it in comparative perspective. Comparative studies of two nations can help provide meaningful general statements about historical patterns and causes. By demonstrating the connections between educational systems and their historical and social contexts, comparative studies can help guard against uncritical borrowing of educational principles and practices; they can also help identify principles and practices that likely could be successfully transplanted.

Harold Silver, in the paper included in this volume (a preliminary report on a larger study still being conducted), hopes to arrive at a general understanding of educational trends by examining the causes and results of educational strategies against poverty in Britain and the United States in the 1960s and 1970s. His comparative historical method differs from a simple historical description of single cases that cannot justify causal statements and from the statistical comparisons of the social sciences that isolate individual "indicators" from their historical setting. Rather, it seeks to determine the factors that led to the different educational policies and to arrive at general statements about causation in particular historical contexts.

This is potentially a very fruitful method, but it is risky since its success depends on the scholar's initial selection of the factors whose causal relevance is to be investigated. Silver avoids the worst pitfalls of this method; he rejects theories that claim that immutable forces, such as the inherent characteristics of capitalism, determined British and American educational policies in the 1960s and 1970s. He is not a determinist of that simple kind. He does not ignore the scope for choices that "objective conditions" frequently leave to the actors in the processes of history. He analyzes the beliefs and values that preceded and accompanied British and American social and educational reform efforts. He holds that values and changes in values offer an important key to understanding the direction educational change might take in a country. Hence the roles of cultural traditions, of dominant or emerging ideas, of political movements, and of creative personalities are examined as factors that could determine the choice between alternative policies in objective situations.

Silver's approach to the study of the relationship of education to poverty rejects the dramatic scenario of failure in favor of a balanced analysis. He adopts a perspective that is not limited by the views either of the educators who formulated the educational policies of the 1960s and 1970s or of their detractors. He questions the ideas of both sides of the debate. He seeks to identify the false premises and the half-truths, and the mistakes in judgment to which they led. But he does not reject out-of-hand the multiple initiatives of those decades. He thinks some of the critics of liberal reform of the 1960s and 1970s have been too judgmental in many of their conclusions, lacking sufficient historical sense of the climate of ideas prevalent at the time. To Silver it is too simple to say that the educational initiatives of the 1960s and 1970s, especially those against poverty, didn't matter, or had it all wrong—or that the fashion is out. He does not give us a catalog of misuses and abuses. He tries to identify the successful contributions as well as the errors of those decades, both of which can enhance future educational strategies.

The relative merits of the social and educational policies of the 1960s and 1970s will no doubt be hotly debated for some time to come. Silver has, with thoroughness and insight, posed questions and laid down some of the terms for any debate that is to ensue.

One of the central issues to be examined for those decades is the relationship between knowledge and power, since educational research occupied a prominent place in educational policy discussions, both substantively and financially. At least two broad conceptions of how knowledge and power interact have been formulated: (1) Knowledge provides an instrument a ruling class can use for its own interests; hence the ruling class, aided by a self-serving ideology, "discovers" knowledge that perpetuates its power. (2) The discovery of a new body of knowledge presents the possibility that a new class of people can emerge and, through institutions of their own making, wield a new kind of power; therefore ideological shifts, which bring with them new value structures, present opportunities for the emergence of a new ruling class. In both formulations knowledge is linked to forms of hegemony.

Michael F.D. Young has been examining hegemonic relationships in education for the last decade, a theme that he explores further in the paper included in this volume. Perhaps more than any other educationist in Britain or the United States during this period, he has demonstrated the relevance of the sociology of knowledge, thought by many scholars to be an arcane and irrelevant branch of sociology, to the sociology of education. In fact, in 1971 he claimed that the sociology of knowledge and the sociology of education were the same branch of intellectual inquiry.

This "new sociology of education," as Young called it, reflected one of the main themes of the 1960s and 1970s—the susceptibility of the methods and findings of science to ideology and to entrenched structures of power. "Knowing" was influenced by the place in historical time and in the social structure of the "knower." According to Young, educational theorists have hypotheses about how children learn, about the relationships of knowledge to individual development and of school to society, that are constantly being revised but are embedded in deeper underlying conceptions from which they are difficult to detach.

We can, I think, infer two levels of "knowledge": a surface level that consists of scientific hypotheses and the findings of educational research; and a deeper level that provides the more elusive denotative framework within which the surface hypotheses get their sense. Taken together these two levels of knowledge fundamentally influence educational practices. Our assumptions and institutions create the phenomena in terms of which we see educational needs and treatments. We classify pupils and put them in special therapeutic centers for "appropriate" treatment by employing categories and systems of our own creation, often with the grim consequences vividly described by Edgar Z. Friedenberg in his paper. Educational research attempts to say what is true and what is false about educational practice, but this activity creates regimes of power—for example, of administrators over teachers, as Young shows in his analysis of the research conducted in Britain by Michael Rutter and his associates; and of teachers over pupils, as Friedenberg shows in his interpretation of research done by Jules Henry and Ray Rist in the United States.

Theorists are not certain that complete detachment of the power of educational research from the forms of hegemony within which it operates in educational institutions is possible. What does seem likely, however, is that power can be reduced or made amenable to control if the potential meanings of ideas, and the conditions that make their extension possible, are carefully analyzed. Therefore, in order to reveal the power that ideology and certain kinds of research exercise over educational practice (wittingly and unwittingly), and to avoid the unwanted effects of that power, Young calls for ethnographical and interpretive sociological studies that open the "black box" of schooling and bring to light what goes on in classrooms; for research initiated by teachers and pupils; for historical research; and for a public debate on the content and control of education.

Throughout the 1960s and 1970s Edgar Z. Friedenberg conducted educational research similar to the ethnographical research Young calls for. Working within the American tradition of classroom observation and micro social science that stretches back at least to Willard Waller's 1932 study of *The Sociology of Teaching*, Friedenberg in several studies examined the effects of the social conditions of classrooms and of teaching styles on the learning of children. His work also examined macrolevels of education and society, for he assumes that the smallest matters of school organization and conduct are influenced by, and reveal, larger patterns of power and control, and the reverse.

Friedenberg's work has helped enlarge the American public's understanding of the special needs of adolescents and youths; and if coming of age in America is less self-destructive, if young people are treated more thoughtfully, and if they can conduct their lives with more dignity today than in the past, it is partly because Friedenberg spoke out determinedly and persuasively on their behalf.

Moreover, the scope of this work has gone beyond education narrowly conceived. Friedenberg has examined authority in its different forms and has demonstrated its sometimes insidious effects on both individuals and groups. He has shown, for example, how authority can sometimes degenerate to a form of exploitation; and he has dextrously used Nietzsche's notion of *ressentiment* to show how exploitation leads simultaneously to the growth of spite and rancour and to the erosion of decency and liberty in ostensibly affluent and democratic nations. He has helped place French sociologist Jacque Ellul's outstanding works explicitly in the center of educational and political debates in the United States; like Ellul, he has argued that technological development produces poverty and inequality, among other products, despite democratic political processes. He has suggested how the enemies of an open society easily can camouflage themselves by adopting the guise of the helping professions and by using the language of therapy. Several of these themes are further explored in his paper in this volume, especially the link between rational and irrational authority and forms of hegemony in Canadian and American schools.

Education in many nations around the world currently is in uneasy but significant transition. Political traditions are being altered in theory and in practice. This is especially true for the nations discussed in this volume—Britain, Canada, and the United States. Changes in educational theory are taking place. There is generally less passion or conviction about what schools can do. The high hopes and promises of the 1960s and 1970s are gone. Education is moving toward something else. The three scholars whose works are included in this volume, all of whom are thoughtful critics of educational research, think research can help guide this evolution of education toward something of greater range and richness than existed in the past. But they all call for changes in the way educational research is conducted. They recommend a chastened form of research, one sensitive to the limitations of time, place, and human constructions; one that leads not only to "rational" and "efficient" decisions but to an increase in meaning and understanding.

During the 1960s and 1970s, educational aims were inflated and generous resources were dissipated. The pretentious language and the dense and rapidly developing political setting made it difficult for educators to separate proposals that had pedagogical merit from those that were merely novel or momentarily seductive. This period of history will leave a clear imprint on whatever follows it. No doubt ideological extravagance in educational discourse and much thoughtlessness in educational practice will continue. Nevertheless, this volume, drawing on another tradition that was kept alive during this period, hopes to help bring about a more chaste discourse and more thoughtful practices.

HAROLD SILVER is author of *Robert Owen on Education, Modern English Society, Equal Opportunity in Education, A Social History of Education in England, The Education of the Poor, English Education and the Radicals—1780-1850, Education and the Social Condition,* and other books. His articles and essays have appeared in *New Society, The Guardian, Times Higher Education Supplement, History of Education, Westminster Studies in Higher Education,* and other periodicals and journals. He formerly was professor of education and social history in the University of London and currently is president of Bulmershe College of Higher Education, Reading, England.

Education Against Poverty: Interpreting British and American Policies in the 1960s and 1970s

Harold Silver

If in the 1970s we had to try to understand and evaluate the disillusionment with and decline of some confident educational policies of the previous decade, in the 1980s we are having to contend with what appear to be fundamental changes of direction. This is now as true of the United States as it has been of Britain since the late 1970s, and the changes in both countries (and not only there) are being carried out partly in the name of revised educational attitudes, more profoundly in the name of economics and public economies. In the 1960s especially, in the United States and in Britain as well as in many European and other countries, education was elevated to a central role in social and economic policy making and planning in pursuit of the ideals of the Welfare State or the War on Poverty or the Great Society or simply social change and the solution of major social problems. In the 1970s, education stood in uncertain light just off center stage. We have begun the 1980s with the scene dominated by a traditionalist or conservative dramatis personae and with education somewhere in the shadows waiting to reappear in the later act of what we do not yet know to be a mystery or a melodrama. We only know it will not be a comedy.

Those of us who had any commitment to the policies or the intentions that began to be formulated and followed in the 1960s must now ask the question: In a year or two, or four or five, shall we go back, start afresh, pick up the pieces, or define new goals? How isolated will surviving policies be from any sense of comprehensive understanding or real direction? If I cannot accept the anti-policies or crudities of the present, how do I rethink the recent past? In the United States, in Australia, and in Britain, I think we have to begin to put the postwar decades into better and more helpful perspective, and there is a real historical job to do in exposing the sources of renewed action. Hope and utopia are not enough. We shall need to be active again before long, not just defensive, in pursuit of a relationship between education and social advance.

Looking back at the education-poverty relationship, then, what are the problems? If Berger and Luckmann and the new sociology, and Michael F.D. Young and the new sociology of education, have taught us anything in the 1970s, it has been the importance and the difficulty of defining the problem—the need to be aware of how knowledge and problems are constructed, who controls them, what structures of power lie behind the question mark. Whoever might claim the theoretical responsibility for defining the problem, I would in fact see this as predominantly a historical issue, though we are all in the business, I think, of deciding what is a theoretical, a sociological, a political, or a historical question or answer. It is important now to build a clear narrative of the 1960s and 1970s, to debate the interpretation, to see what choices have been and remain available, and what new pressures are building up around us. From the perspectives of a research project only just begun, I would like to focus on the 1960s in Britain and the United States, and underline some problems of conducting the retrospect.[1]

A poverty-education connection is a nineteenth as well as a twentieth century phenomenon. At various stages of the past two centuries that relationship has been defined with a variety of emphases. It has been interpreted as an ethical relationship, with education being called to social rescue, to induce right behavior, to help the victims of social change to accept old or modified values. It has been an economic relationship, expressed in terms of the contribution of education to manpower provision, or to the containment of public expenditure (for example, in the form of the cheapness of schools as compared with the public bill for crime and prisons). The relationship has been expressed in political terms, with education being asked to reinforce social stability as new electorates have entered the country or won political suffrage. The relationship has been expressed in both radical and conservative terms, and the ensuing educational and social policies have been defined and interpreted in terms of both—often barely separable. The distance between the conservative hope that education protects an old order, and the radical hope of educational contributions to social improvement and reorganization, in fact, has not always been easy to establish.

In the past two centuries the education-poverty relationship has been underlined at points that can be plotted along different kinds of axes—demographic, economic, industrial—and none of the graphs of the timing and the rhythm of the connection have yet proved entirely satisfactory—though recent work in the United States by Kaestle and Vinovskis, and by Tyack and his colleagues, has been revealing and helpful.[2] What is clear is that the connection, real or intended, has been associated with the rhythm at which poverty has been discovered and rediscovered in both countries in the past two centuries. The awareness of the extent and concentration of poverty in Britain in the industrializing period of the late eighteenth and early nineteenth centuries, the heightened awareness of poverty and its implications resulting in the midnineteenth century from the writings of Mayhew, at the end of the nineteenth century from the researches of Booth and Rowntree, and the rediscovery of chronic poverty by British sociologists such as Titmuss, Audrey Harvey, and Willmott and Young in the 1950s and 1960s relate to the reemergence of education as a central policy instrument in various forms. They directed attention both toward poverty and toward its apparent effects.

In a variety of ways education has also been linked with poverty over the past two centuries at times of heightened public consciousness of the need to protect the social order by reasserting ideal social and national types. This has been true of periods of immigration and social tension, and—as in the 1960s—during periods of what appear to be potentially difficult or sensitive social changes. All of those linkages between education and poverty are incomplete and even misleading as explanations, since at the same time education has become an autonomous demand, an ideal, a right, a claim as a cultural or economic asset. The relationship is therefore too complex and fluid to subordinate to some simple social control theory. If the nineteenth century established education as a central social mechanism, it also witnessed its emergence as a constantly changing battlefield. There is no one simple and straightforward explanation of the confidence of a Horace Mann or a Lyndon Johnson, of a Robert Owen or an Anthony Crosland, in education as a basic strategy for eradicating poverty.

What, if anything, was new and different about the emphases and strategies and definitions of the 1960s? It is useful to begin with the United States and to look at the context in which the rediscovery of the education-poverty relationship in postwar America took place. The central thrusts of the rediscovery were expressed in terms of a new and more effective federal politics of education, new forms of intervention through education, a new scale of funding and newly defined target populations, a new concentration of interest in disadvantage, and a conjoint interest in community action and compensatory strategies.

The context out of which the range of policies emerged, especially from 1964, included the growing federal interest in educational policymaking in conditions of the cold war and technological change—symbolized by the space race that began with sputnik in 1957 and the passing of the National Defense Education Act the following year. The context included, perhaps most of all, the civil rights movement of the late 1950s and the new militancies, public action, and orchestration of demands and policies that accompanied and grew out of it. It is against that background that poverty began to be rediscovered, conceptualized, and translated into political terms by President Kennedy and his close associates in the period 1962-64. Up to this point there had been a widespread belief in both the United States and Europe that poverty as a major social issue, and defined as such, had been cured or had gone away. As a significant issue, and expressed in that vocabulary and form, poverty surfaced as a political issue only in 1964.[3] Sundquist commented in 1969:

> Lyndon Johnson had added the word "poverty" for the first time to the lexicon of recognized public problems when he proclaimed, "This administration today, here and now, declares unconditional war on poverty in America." Until 1964, the word "poverty" did not appear as a heading in the index of either the *Congressional Record* or *The Public Papers of the President.*[4]

For the previous two years the Kennedy administration had been seeking its new frontiers, and Kennedy's experience of Appalachian poverty had contributed to a heightened sense of social policy involvement. The familiar story of Kennedy's reading of Michael Harrington's *The Other America* is neither apocryphal nor trivial, and there is clear evidence that that book, together with the seminal review of it by Dwight McDonald, captured a moment of awareness and urgency and made its dimensions politically accessible.[5] Harrington himself was to be invited to take part in the first poverty program task force. By 1962-64 a number of factors were beginning to coincide and to provide the basis on which Johnson was to act after Kennedy's assassination.

One important element in interpreting the growing interest in poverty and education as related issues is the emphasis that many analysts have placed on the absence of any serious direct link between the poverty interest and major public pressures, including the civil rights movement itself. In the period preceding 1964 there were, it is true, no discernible pressures for anything that could be described as a poverty program. The unemployment rate was low, the poor were unorganized and were, in Murphy's words, making "no demands for such legislation."[6] Yarmolinsky, writing in 1969, described the 1964 task force that planned the Economic Opportunity Act as issuing a number of memoranda, one of which was entitled "Why the Poverty Program is Not a Negro Program." This was

> devoted primarily to the fact that the poverty problem in Appalachia and the Ozarks was almost entirely a white problem and the Deep South was a white as well as a Negro problem. The crisis of the northern ghetto was simply not foreseen in anything like its present critical character by the draftsmen of the program.[7]

In determining the roots of educational policies in the 1960s, and of any other policies, of course, it has to be remembered that foresight does not have to be clear—vague messages, memories, and fears can be translated into political action and social policy, as the history of inner-city issues, for example, often shows. However, in the absence of a clear relationship between popular pressure and the Johnson declaration of war on poverty, some analysts have also looked to the debates of the late 1950s and early 1960s for other sources of ideal and energy and have found, for example, a major starting point in the discussions of juvenile delinquency, with which Robert Kennedy was particularly associated.[8] Others have seen the 1964 programs as coming at a "pause" in the civil rights movement and have emphasized its likely regrouping and renewal as part of the consciousness underlying the Great Society rhetoric. The poverty program, claimed Raab in 1965, was "part and parcel of the Negro revolution, of the direct action demonstrations and anarchic ghetto restlessness."[9]

What is clear is that the succession of education bills that had ended nowhere in previous sessions of Congress had not been linked directly to poverty. The 1963 National Education Improvement Bill, for example, when discussed in the House Committee on Education and Labor, raised, like so many previous bills, issues to do with federal aid to the states, vocational education, higher education opportunities, and so on, but was not directed toward a specific target population.[10] The language, concepts, and linkages of 1964-65 are altogether different. They embody a number of factors that, coming together, rapidly announced the presence of a new consciousness, new emphases, and the launching of a new rhetoric. They contain elements of civil rights and desegregation, of the political objectives of Kennedy and Johnson and their close associates, and also of the newly and rapidly emerging ideas and research and experience of work being promoted by some of the foundations, notably the Ford Foundation, with people like Ylvisaker from the latter quickly contributing to the new movement. The result was "an interacting sequence of theory, experiment, and demonstration that produced new strategic and tactical concepts for what became the War on Poverty."[11]

It was on that basis that the Economic Opportunity Act was passed in 1964, authorizing expenditures that produced Head Start in 1965 and Follow Through two years later. This was the basis of Title I of the Elementary and Secondary Education Act of 1965 (ESEA), part of a wide-ranging attack on the "root causes of poverty in the midst of plenty" and representing the widely held belief that poverty, having been discovered, would now soon be abolished.[12]

The year 1964 was the beginning of a brief heroic period in which ideas were debated, advice taken, task forces established, drafting done, policies defined and canvassed, and legislation enacted.[13] It was soon to become clear that the confident and specific strategies in many cases postponed or disguised old conflicts and confusions and that expectations and expansionist educational aims had in many cases been dressed in extravagant stage costume. For Hubert Humphrey education had become "the key to the door through which the poor can escape from poverty."[14] For Johnson the problem was not one of income redistribution: the American people "are going to learn their way out of poverty."[15] In May 1964 Johnson told the students of the University of Michigan:

> In your time we have the opportunity to move not only toward the rich society and the powerful society, but upward to the Great Society. The Great Society . . . demands an end to poverty and racial injustice, to which we are totally committed in our time. But that is just the beginning. The Great Society is a place where every child can find knowledge to enrich his mind and to enlarge his talents . . . It is a place where the city of man serves not only the needs of the body and the demands of commerce, but the desire for beauty and the hunger for community.[16]

The New Republic liked that enough to reprint it in a book entitled *America Tomorrow: Creating the Great Society*. The dismissal of all or any of this as mere rhetoric, or idealism gone sour, or political opportunism, or whatever, does not help. This was an important American moment that has to be understood, and the roles of the newly conceptualized poverty and the educational war against it, its extent, its targets, and its limitations, have to be disentangled and evaluated as the decisions of real people responding to real imperatives and choices.

The British narrative and its component parts begin quite differently. If there was a heroic period it has to be a much earlier one, surrounding the publication of the 1942 Beveridge Report on postwar social security, the drafting and publication of the 1944 Education Act, and the period immediately following the war, with the election of the Attlee Labor government, and the enactment of a series of legislative concerns with health, welfare, and nationalization.

The British moment, if you like, was one that used a vocabulary of construction and planning, and public ownership and control, not warfare. The goals were expressed in terms of the ending of a remembered, prewar experience of widespread unemployment and poverty, and the legislation was in part a socialist commitment, in part a set of wartime promises redeemed. The problem of the 1960s in Britain was one of increasing realization that the postwar measures had been cloaked in a fair measure of idealism, and that serious underlying problems remained.

The rediscovery of poverty was an important feature of British social policy and social administration in the 1950s, and related directly to social-class analysis, the influential interpretation of working-class culture conducted by Richard Hoggart, and the community-directed sociology that emanated outstandingly from the Institute of Community Studies. Poverty was rediscovered in a context quite different from the pressures and concerns of 1950s America.

A second and crucial discovery in 1950s Britain was that education, as embodied in legislation and practice, had not made the expected inroads into the class structure. The implementation of the 1920s and 1930s slogan "secondary education for all" under the 1944 Education Act had not significantly affected the distribution of education and social opportunity as perceived at the time in, for example, access to grammer school, to academically oriented examinations, and to higher education. The sociologists mustered by David Glass in the early- and mid-1950s, the crucially influential *Social Class and Educational Opportunity* by Floud, Halsey and Martin in 1956, and the increasing importance of the sociology of education had by the 1960s altered the pattern of public discussion and redirected public attention.

Whatever the later criticisms of their definitions and theoretical positions, the sociologists of the 1950s and 1960s profoundly altered the agenda of social policy discussion. They made social class, as a concept and a set of issues, as basic to the British debates of the 1960s as race had become for the United States.

The focus of educational discussion in the mid-1960s, especially after the election of Harold Wilson's Labor government in 1964, was the comprehensive school. The discussion did not point directly toward the concept of poverty, but it did so obliquely as a concern with social justice, fairness, equality of access, and educational efficiency and opportunity. By the late 1950s and early 1960s, however, other forms of social and political action and ideal had begun to shape discussion of all forms of social policy. The Campaign for Nuclear Disarmament and the New Left made their impact on a whole range of discussions that had for a long time been seen as outside the concerns of popular politics, and the issues of education and poverty were beneficiaries of newly released energies of this kind. In addition, by the end of the 1950s the profile of the British social structure had begun to alter significantly. The newly defined problems of affluent youth and adolescents were obviously not far from any discussion of education. The main period of West Indian, Asian, and African immigration was during the late 1950s. By the 1960s sharper awareness was beginning to be expressed of the stresses of the inner city, of concentrations of poverty, of social problems, of crime, of the anxieties of an increasingly pluralist society. The policies which were sought and adopted did not necessarily coincide, as was also true of the United States, with moments of great economic or political pressures, but they certainly related to a sense of potential and major causes for concern. As in the United States, although to a lesser degree, the new policies were formulated in expansionist and confident terms, though British politicians and government commissions expressed themselves more guardedly than their counterparts in the United States!

A 1963 Advisory Council report on pupils "of average and less than average ability" (the definition of the terms of reference is interesting) contained a chapter on "Education in the Slums".[17] The Robbins Committee on higher education in the same year drew heavily on the work of the sociologists to demonstrate that working-class children were not being recruited adequately to advanced secondary and higher education.[18] The Plowden Committee of 1963-67 on children and their primary schools soon followed, with its emphasis on positive discrimination and Educational Priority Areas, and on forms of educational and social action not unlike those of mid-1960s America. Of all the reports, Plowden placed the poverty-education relationship most firmly at the center of its concerns.[19]

By the second half of the 1960s a remarkable convergence of definitions, vocabulary, research, and policy formulation had taken place between Britain and the United States, even if the scale of implementation was vastly dissimilar. The contexts, starting points, national structures, and public issues were incredibly different, and historically they cannot be dismissed as merely different expressions of underlying dilemmas of varieties of capitalist society. American liberalism is not the same as British social democracy, and neither of them is homogeneous. It is not helpful, historically, to attempt to write off the two sets of transatlantic actors as puppets manipulated by the same demon or underlying force.

It is not possible here to itemize in detail the British and American policies that emerged within such a short space of time in the middle and late 1960s, but it is important to underline the general pattern. In the United States between 1964 and 1967 the Economic Opportunity Act authorized federal expenditure for a variety of purposes connected explicitly with poverty and launched the processes that quickly resulted in community action programs and Head Start. With doubts about the gains being made by Head Start children being sustained in the elementary school, President Johnson authorized Follow Through in 1967, a project poised uncertainly between a service model to supplement Head Start and an experimental, developmental model to improve early schooling.[20] From 1965, Title I of ESEA operated through the states, but federal funding and guidelines as to target populations and expenditures, and federal monitoring of action by the states, brought poverty and educational policy centrally into a new profile of federal action. Job Corps, Vista, Upward Bound,and an enormous number of related federal,state, and local projects that followed the Economic Opportunity Act of 1964, publically and privately funded, rapidly made new strategies and vocabularies familiar, with the concept of compensatory education at the center of the exercise.

In Britain, from 1964 to the end of the decade, the move toward comprehensive reorganization centered on government circular 10/65 that put pressure on local authorities to submit reorganization plans to end selection at the age of eleven and establish the comprehensive secondary school. This was the period of the peak of research and publication regarding the relationship between social class and the family on the one hand, and the school on the other.[21] The Plowden Report proposed its policy of positive discrimination in favor of children in poor environments, and its recommendation for the designation of Educational Priority Areas (EPA) was acted upon. EPA action research projects were funded and were to produce, in 1972, 1974, and 1975, the most notable reports on British compensatory (or complementary, as the project organizers preferred) educational schemes on anything like a scale that can be compared with the American experience.[22] The use of Urban Aid money for preschool purposes from 1969 and the establishment of a National Community Development Project in 1970 completed a picture that at many points resembled the American one.

While Washington was busy in the 1960s with academics and specialists of many kinds, advising the federal government and its agencies on the whole range of educational concerns, London was, though to a much more limited extent, bringing together the British equivalents to advise the parties (in this context mostly the Labor party), and to talk to publishers. In Britain this was the great age of the literature of education, disadvantage, and deprivation; of the comprehensive school; of education and social change; of education and social class; and of sociolinguistics, education and streaming, testing, and selecting.

There are immediate points about all of this to underline. First, the American experience, especially from 1964, attracted substantial attention and large numbers of inquiring visitors from the United Kingdom. A. H. Halsey, with J. Floud and C. A. Anderson, made some of the early American literature widely known in Britain.[23] The Ford Foundation and the Organization for Economic Control and Development arranged a conference in the United States in January 1969 at which European participants could explore the issues with some of their American counterparts;[24] and Marris and Rein published a well-known account of poverty and community action in the United States.[25] Members of the Plowden Committee visited the United States to see and discuss some of the American developments. The Plowden Report makes only rare reference to the American projects, but the report is extensively constructed in ways that suggest what was learned from across the Atlantic. Halsey's 1972 report on the EPA projects contains a chapter on "Poverty and American Compensatory Education." The fortunes of Head Start and its evaluations were as familiar to British educationists as they were to Americans. Although the American desegregation and busing issues were followed attentively in Britain, they had little echo by comparison with the poverty programs.

Two aspects of British experience transmitted important messages in the reverse direction. First, the British infant school, the "open classroom" and "progressive education" attracted incredible postwar American interest and were as important to the transatlantic airlines as the American programs were. The infant classroom was widely, if not always realistically, reported in the United States, and its apparent "informal" methodology was incorporated into some of the "planned variation" models available to Head Start and Follow Through children.[26] Second, the British sociology of education and social class had important echoes in the United States, both in the 1960s and then in the radical review it encountered at the beginning of the 1970s, most notably in the volume on

Knowledge and Control edited by Michael F. D. Young.[27] The outstanding contribution to the American developments was that of Basil Bernstein, whose early work on working-class and middle-class language "codes" was widely used by influential early-childhood and education specialists in the mid-1960s. Deutsch, for example, used Bernstein's work in 1964 to explain "the communication gap which can exist between the middle-class teacher and the lower-class child," and Deutsch's whole vocabulary of class analysis was probably influenced by Bernstein.[28] Bereiter and Engelmann used Bernstein in support of their approach to *Teaching Disadvantaged Children in the Preschool* in 1966 and in developing the idea of an "academically oriented preschool for culturally deprived children."[29]

The various kinds of interchange contributed, of course, to the shared confidence and the shared sense of a major shift in public attitudes to social issues and their educational implications. The vocabulary of "disadvantage" and "compensatory education" and "cultural deprivation" was shared initially with confidence and then increasingly with uncertainty, as attacks were mounted on the concepts of "cultural deprivation" and "compensatory education" on both sides of the Atlantic.[30] Shared confidence inevitably meant shared disappointments, shared debate, shared confusion. What, after all, *was* poverty? What did the concepts and the policies actually mean when stripped of their expansionist economic assumptions? Was it possible to discuss the education-poverty relationship without imposing middle-class values? What, in Atlanta or Liverpool, did "maximum feasible participation of the poor" or similar phraseology really mean?[31] What implications for policy were there in the Westinghouse evaluation of Head Start, or in the Coleman Report, or in Jencks' *Inequality?*

Alongside all of this kind of sharing, we have to remember other elements of it. Britain was sharing with other West European countries, including Germany, France, and Sweden, attempts to restructure secondary education under pressures for democratization. The American and British issues were discussed in European forums, and underpinned the interests of the OECD. Australia has been discovering poverty and the British and American experience.

The questions of interpretation that arise from all of this are obviously extremely difficult. The most contentious of the interpretations has related to outcomes, and the problems can be expressed in three ways.

First, they have to do with the difficulties of evaluation. It is clear, for example, that between 1965 and 1974 the available evaluations of ESEA Title I were of little or no value, since the lack of proper guidelines, experience, and standardization meant that the data produced were unusable. The results were (1) the mandate in 1974 to the National Institute of Education to conduct its Compensatory Education Study, and (2) the contract with System Development Corporation to conduct the still ongoing Sustaining Effects Study. Neither of these has had the notoriety of earlier evaluations of, for example, Head Start and Follow Through, since their results have been more positive and encouraging. The difficulties encountered by evaluators in interpreting some of the data, especially in the late 1960s and early 1970s, will make it difficult for historians to see much of the evaluation produced as helpful in making serious interpretations of the projects and their outcomes.

Second, and directly related to the former, are measurement difficulties. Since the 1966 Coleman Report, it has been difficult to understand what kind of measures are appropriate as well as really indicative. Measurement techniques have been used that are not only controversial within the scholarly community, but are also based on criteria that have too often been taken for granted. The comment has been endlessly made that cognitive measures are neither as reliable as often claimed, nor indicative of more than a fraction of the outcomes, intended and unintended, with which educational processes are concerned. In relation to Follow Through, for example, one of the sponsors has pointed out major areas, such as motivation and parent involvement, that are ignored by the measures and the intentions of those designing and using them.[32] One local Follow Through project organizer has commented that the project has had to make a constant effort to try to persuade people to understand "that everything we do is not measurable by standardized tests, that things that you do with the child for positive self-concept—you can't measure that on a standardized test."[33]

The measurement obsessions of the 1960s and 1970s may be judged by historians to have been a feature of the sophisticated arrogance of a primitive science. Jack Tizard and his colleagues in Britain stressed in *All Our Children* that nursery education had to do with happiness, well-being, and the development of children and their families, with relatively immediate goals, not with hoped-for and measurable long-term effects.[34] I think this whole formulation is unsatisfactory, but given the history of measurement processes and uses in the past decade or more I understand and sympathize with it.

Third, the difficulties can be described in terms of the concern with overall impact. If education is to be used to combat poverty, then clearly some sort of assessment of effectiveness is necessary, and social class, social mobility, and intra- and inter-generational studies are important. But modesty and caution have been sadly lacking. An example is a sentence from Jencks' *Inequality* which suggests that the "egalitarian trend in education has not made the distribution of income or status appreciably more equal over the past 25 years."[35] I no longer believe that to be a legitimate pronouncement, given the extent and nature of the resources and the methodology available to the researchers. Or even if there are grounds on which to make judgments about social mobility, status distribution, and income trends over such a period, to make them with the confidence that suggests the impossibility of change does not seem to be appropriate to that kind of exercise. That is the prerogative of politician, political theorist, and hunch.

We should have been more hesitant about all of this, as some people have tried to be recently in Britain—about, for example, Bennett's or the Oracle Project work on teaching styles and pupil performance, or Rutter's *15,000 Hours*. But too many people on the right and on the left were only too eager in the late 1960s and 1970s to use the evidence of an immature science to support bold interpretations. Bowles and Gintis, for example, used it to proclaim gleefully that "the liberal school-reform bubble has burst . . . The disappointing results of the War on Poverty . . . have decisively discredited liberal social policy." They quoted approvingly a judgment from the Rand Corporation that "virtually without exception all of the large surveys of the large national compensatory educational programs have shown no beneficial results on the average.[36]

There is now a different picture that could be drawn of the effects of the educational programs against poverty—not in order to suggest that it is the *true* picture as against the *false* picture presented by the negative evaluations, but in order to suggest that many, like Bowles and Gintis, leaped too enthusiastically into accepting initial evaluations as gospel. There are at least ten sources for an alternative picture of the outcomes of the projects conceived in the 1960s and 1970s. In the United States, for example, the National Institute of Education (NIE) Compensatory Education Study pointed out the redistributive effects of Title I, the positive data relating to student gains in first and third grades, and the fact that students making such gains on compensatory programs did not then slip back. The Executive Summary of the evaluation is a crucial set of positive statements to set against the earlier and more publicized negative evaluations.[37] The same is true of the reports produced by the Sustaining Effects Study from the second half of the 1970s. Barbara Heyns, one of Jencks' collaborators on the *Inequality* study, has in *Summer Learning and the Effects of Schooling* (1978) offered a more optimistic view of the effects of public education than previous literature in the same investigative mold. She concludes:

> Schooling has a substantial independent effect on the achievement of children and . . . the outcomes resulting from schooling are far more equal than those that would be expected based on the social class and racial origins of sámple children. . . . Although achievement differences persist, and schools cannot be regarded as equalizing in an absolute sense, the pattern of outcomes clearly implies that the achievement gap between children of diverse backgrounds are attenuated by education.[38]

In his foreword to Heyns' book, and in his own more recent work, Jencks takes a less assertive position than previously on the possible effects of education.[39] Also in the United States the Consortium of fourteen infant and preschool experiments reanalysed from 1975 the preschool programs that had been the subject of much previous analysis and debate. The outcomes of the work of the Consortium teams pointed to the effectiveness of some preschool programs on a number of significant criteria: "The most important finding is that low-income children who received early education are better able to meet the minimal requirements of their schools as shown in a reduced rate of assignment to special education and in-grade retention."[40]

Some recent analyses of the Follow Through programs have come to quite different conclusions about their effectiveness than did earlier analyses.[41]

In Britain, the first EPA report by A. H. Halsey in 1972 suggested some more positive conclusions than the American literature had about the possibility of sustained gains by preschool children on compensatory programs. Although the evidence from the London EPA published three years later was less optimistic, other evidence from the projects, especially from West Riding, suggested cautiously optimistic outcomes.[42] A recent book by Halsey, Heath, and Ridge on *Origins and Destinations* concludes that the record of educational policy-making does not point to easy optimism, but also indicates that it does not endorse defeatism either.[43] The *15,000 Hours* study by Rutter and his colleagues suggests that differences in student performance can be attributed to certain kinds of difference in the schools.[44] Although in relation to this study, as to other items in this list, there are methodological and other reservations to be expressed, the cumulative effect of all of these American and British studies is to leave wide open questions that earlier evaluations considered to be closed. Whether it is yet possible to share the confidence of the title of Halsey's 1980 article, "Education Can Compensate," is not clear, but it reflects some of the changed emphases that have emerged since Basil Bernstein wrote his 1972 article in the same journal under the title "Education Cannot Compensate for Society."[45] We are still, as we should have understood much earlier, at the infancy of evaluative procedures.

Are there any conclusions about these antipoverty policies and programs, given the present state of our knowledge and analysis? The existing literature that attempts to look back over the 1960s and 1970s experience seems to me to fall into three rough categories in both Britain and the United States. The first is the description and analysis that comes from what the contributors might consider some kind of "objective center," handling the actors on more or less their own terms, probing their meanings, and exposing their interactions. Some of it is autobiographical, or accounts of witnesses at the center or the periphery of the events. Some of it emanates from the evaluative tradition built up in the 1960s and 1970s, and much of it is more in the tradition of portraiture and landscape painting than sustained analysis. A great deal of it is invaluable as source material, as perceptions that check and balance one another, and is of major importance to the historian, without itself being history.

The second category is profoundly judgmental, often of the very attempt to bring education into a political and social arena, and embraces a politically right-wing perspective. This has until recently been less articulate, less raucous, and less influential in the United States than in Britain, because this position has been less easy to occupy in the face of major public issues in the United States, especially those connected with race. It has been visible, nevertheless, in some contributions to *Public Interest* and *Commentary* and has been most clearly and directly embodied in the Heritage Foundation's 1980 report to then President-elect Reagan, proposing, for example, that programs should not be funded "which foster hostility to traditional values, or which unquestioningly accept moral relativism as an ethical theory." The emphasis in the report is on federal aid but also on the withdrawal of federal control and, for example, on the ending of affirmative action. It proposes that all federal agencies should be staffed by individuals who "oppose any further Federal support for 'humanistic' or psycho-social education, activities, projects or programs."[46] This is the American equivalent of the British *Black Papers,* which from 1969 sought to expunge the record of the previous decade and were less concerned with appraising that experience than with asserting the need to return to older, traditional, understood, tried, and tested academic and cultural values.

Third, on the political left there have often been equally assertive and declamatory positions: Marxist, anarchist, radical. The best-known British version has been Finn, Grant, and Johnson's paper on "Social Democracy, Education and the Crisis," describing "an educational system under siege" and the growth of a ruling class-dominated educational ideology and structure.[47] The key text in Britain and the United States, however, has been Bowles and

Gintis' *Schooling in Capitalist America,* with its underlying message of an almost inescapable trap for educators and reformers in capitalist society. Reforms have in the main, in this argument, been manipulative, reactive, and compromising. The open classroom, they suggest, was "perceived by liberal educators as a means of accommodating and circumscribing the growing antiauthoritarianism of young people and keeping things from getting out of hand." The history of twentieth-century education "is the history not of Progressivism but of the imposition upon the schools of 'business values.'" Education has historically played the role not of a complement to economic reform, but as a substitute for it. Education "plays a major role in hiding or justifying the exploitative nature of the U.S. economy."[48] Whatever grains of truth might lie in any of this, these are political assertions masquerading as history. Bowles and Gintis *needed* the 1960s reforms, like any other reforms, to be seen to have failed, and they rushed into accepting evaluations and judgments and data from sources, such as Rand, which for other purposes and in other circumstances they would have resisted and rejected. Their argument ends in the same trap as does that of Martin Carnoy, for example, in 1976, when he insists that "fundamental changes in schooling . . . will require fundamental changes in the basic structures of the society"—apparently inviting educators to maximum apathy and inaction, since as long as our present "basic structures" remain intact there is no point whatever in trying to alter anything.[49] Henry Levin, looking at European secondary school reform, in 1978 saw the tensions arising from these reforms producing frustrated expectations that would result in postponing the tensions to the higher education stage. As a result,

> it is likely that these frustrations and feelings of dissatisfaction with both the educational system and the labor market will lead to increasing manifestations of class conflict and struggle. Individual incidents of sabotage by frustrated and underemployed workers, rising political activism by the unemployed, and other forms of disruption such as strikes (both on and off campus) are likely to increase as it becomes evident that appropriate jobs will not be forthcoming, even in the distant future.

Levin goes on to underline his conclusions from the European experience of school reorganization in previous decades:

> Political demands for worker control of enterprises and nationalization of industry as well as increased public employment are likely to besiege both firms and governments. Coalitions of radicalized workers and students will contribute to the rising instabilities of the liberal, capitalist, Western European countries by pushing for egalitarian changes . . . [50]

This is assertion, without roots in historical analysis (not even Levin's own) of the experience apparently under discussion. In its approach to the kind of phenomena with which we are dealing in the 1960s and 1970s, it ultimately produces nothing more than an alternative, inhibiting rhetoric.

To historians all of this ideologically inspired rhetoric is a familiar problem, only this time expressed in terms of relatively recent events. In relation to historical processes in general, historians frequently have to face the dilemma of contemporaneous and postfacto judgments. They can accept and record the actors' own accounts of their actions and the events in which they were participants or witnesses, acknowledging that such accounts are likely to have recognizable partialities, prejudices, and limitations. Or they can introduce into their accounts and analyses the consciousness of "underlying forces" which were not perceived by, were unknown to, were not accessible to the actors themselves. The difficulty in this case is that ultimately history may be left behind altogether in favor of speculative theory. Whatever Bowles and Gintis, Carnoy and Levin, and Finn, Grant and Johnson are doing in their discussions of and assertions about liberalism, capitalism, and social democracy, it is not history. If what they are doing is theory, it points all the more strongly to the need for more sustained and sensitive ways of conducting a dialogue between theory and history, and this cannot be done on the basis of rhetorical, assertive theory from the left or the right, especially if it purports to be history or to be grounded in historical analysis.

It is obviously no easier to find solutions and to conduct acceptable historical analyses in terms of the 1960s than it has been in interpreting policy and reform in the late nineteenth and early twentieth centuries. Instead of abandoning the period and the field to autobiography and memoirs or to comparisons with better, hoped-for utopias, we need to look hard at the complex motivation behind the 1960s developments, at the diverse meanings on both sides of the education-poverty relationship, at the possible outcomes, at the ways we have evaluated and judged in the past, at the real choices available then and now, at the possibilities of renewed and effective action. It is all the more important to think in these terms and to deal with the significant recent past in such ways, since our capacity for renewed and effective action may depend on them. It is important, similarly, to see beyond our limited national experience and to be aware of the utility and the difficulties of approaching the converging and diverging elements in other versions of similar issues. Having shared in many ways our 1960s and 1970s experience, there seems to be enormous virtue in continuing to share the experience of the hazards already so visible in both Britain and the United States.

FOOTNOTES

1. British and American Educational Strategies Against Poverty in the 1960s and 1970s, a project funded by the Social Science Research Council (UK), 1980-82.

2. Carl F. Kaestle and Maris A. Vinovskis, *Education and Social Change in Nineteenth-Century Massachusetts* (Cambridge, Cambridge University Press, 1980); John W. Meyer et al., "Public Education as Nation-Building in America: Enrollments and Bureaucratization in the American States, 1870-1930," *American Journal of Sociology*, vol. 85, no. 3 (1979).

3. Byron G. Lander, "Group Theory and Individuals: The Origin of Poverty as a Political Issue in 1964," *The Western Political Quarterly*, vol. 24, no. 3 (1971), p. 154; Theodore R. Sizer, "Low-Income Families and the Schools for their Children." *Public Administration Review*, vol. 30, no. 4 (1970), p. 340.

4. James L. Sundquist, "Origins of the War on Poverty," in James L. Sundquist, ed., *On Fighting Poverty: Perspectives from experience* (New York, Basic Books, 1969), p. 6.

5. Lander, "Group Theory and Individuals," pp. 519-520; Adam Yarmolinsky, "The Beginnings of OEO," in Sundquist, *On Fighting Poverty*, p. 38; Sundquist, "Origins of the War on Poverty," p. 7.

6. Jerome T. Murphy, "Title I of ESEA: The Politics of Implementing Federal Education Reform," *Harvard Educational Review*, vol. 41, no. 1, pp. 37-8. For a detailed discussion of this theme see Lawrence M. Friedman, "The Social and Political Context of the War on Poverty: An Overview," in Robert H. Haveman, ed., *A Decade of Federal Antipoverty Programs: Achievements, failures and lessons* (New York, Academic Press, 1977). See also Sundquist, "Origins of the War on Poverty" for a similar account which does not tackle the issue explicitly, and also Lander, "Group Theory and Individuals," pp. 514-517.

7. Yarmolinsky, "The Beginnings of OEO," p. 42.

8. Sundquist, "Origins of the War on Poverty," p. 11; Lander, "Group Theory and Individuals," pp. 512-513.

9. Earl Raab, "What War and Which Poverty?," *The Public Interest*, no. 1 (1965), pp. 46, 56.

10. National Education Improvement Act. Hearings before the Committee on Education and Labor, House of Representatives . . . on H.R. 3000, Washington D.C., 1963.

11. Sundquist, "Origins of the War on Poverty," pp. 9, 19.

12. Murphy, "Title I of ESEA," p. 37.

13. Thomas E. Cronin, "The Presidency and Education," *Phi Delta Kappan*, vol. 49, no. 6 (1968), pp. 295-6.

14. Hubert H. Humphrey, *War on Poverty* (New York, McGraw-Hill, 1964), p. 141.

15. Quoted by Charles I. Norris, Introduction to Nelson F. Ashline *et al.*, eds., *Education, Inequality and National Policy* (Lexington, Mass., D.C. Heath), p. xvii.

16. "America Tomorrow: Creating the Great Society," *The New Republic*, 1965, p. 41.

17. Ministry of Education, *Half Our Future*, a report of the Central Advisory Council for Education (London, HMSO, 1963).

18. Committee on Higher Education, *Higher Education: Report* (London, HMSO, 1963).

19. Department of Education and Science, *Children and their Primary Schools*, a report of the Central Advisory Council for Education (London, HMSO, 1967).

20. The literature on Follow Through and other compensatory projects is enormous. See, for example, Joan S. Bissell, "Planned Variation in Head Start and Follow Through," in Julian C. Stanley, ed., *Compensatory Education for Children, Ages 2 to 8: Recent studies of educational intervention* (Baltimore, Johns Hopkins University Press, 1973).

21. The best known example of this literature in Britain was J.W.B Douglas, *The Home and the School: A study of ability and attainment in the primary schools* (London, MacGibbon and Kee, 1964).

22. Department of Education and Science, *Educational Priority*, report of a research project sponsored by the Department of Education and Science and the Social Science Research Council, 5 vols (London, HMSO, 1972-75).

23. A.H. Halsey, Jean Floud, and C. Arnold Anderson, *Education, Economy and Society: A reader in the sociology of education* (New York, Free Press, 1961).

24. Alan Little and George Smith, *Strategies of Compensation: A review of educational projects for the disadvantaged in the United States*. The British participants were A.H. Halsey, and the two authors of this review, the latter of whom was also an EPA project organizer. See also Schools Council Working Paper 27, *Cross'd With Adversity* (London, Evans/Methuen, 1970), for similar evidence of awareness of the American experience.

25. Peter Marris and Martin Rein, *Dilemmas of Social Reform: Poverty and community action in the United States* (London, Routledge and Kegan Paul, 1967).

26. See Bissell, "Planned Variation in Head Start and Follow Through."

27. Michael F.D. Young, ed., *Knowledge and Control: New directions for the sociology of education* (London, Collier Macmillan, 1971). See also Richard Brown, ed., *Knowledge, Education, and Cultural Change: Papers in the sociology of education* (London, Tavistock, 1973).

28. See Fred M. Hechinger, ed., *Pre-School Education Today* (New York, Doubleday), pp. 88, 13.

29. Carl Bereiter and S. Engelmann, *Teaching Disadvantaged Children in the Preschool* (Englewood Cliffs, New Jersey, Prentice-Hall, 1966), pp. 32-33.

30. The seminal article in Britain was Basil Bernstein's "Education Cannot Compensate for Society," *New Society*, February 26, 1970. An important book was Nell Keddie, ed., *Tinker, Tailor . . . The Myth of Cultural Deprivation* (Harmondsworth, England, Penguin, 1973) (the subtitle was used as the title in the American Penguin edition of the same year). A strong, direct attack was mounted by William Ryan in 1971 (Ch 2: "Savage Discovery in the Schools: The folklore of cultural deprivation").

31. Daniel P. Moynihan, *Maximum Feasible Misunderstanding: Community action in the war on poverty* (New York, Free Press, 1969). The participatory nature of the community school in the Liverpool EPA project is probably the nearest British educational equivalent to the American intentions after 1964. See Eric Midwinter, *Priority Education: An account of the Liverpool project*, (Harmondsworth, England, Penguin, 1972)(Ch. 1: "The Solution: The Community School.")

32. Walter Hodges, "The Worth of the Follow Through Experience," *Harvard Educational Review*, vol. 48, no. 2 (1978).

33. Interview with Mrs. Fay Ross, Atlanta Schools Follow Through Project, Atlanta, Georgia, April 1981.

34. Jack Tizard, et al., *All Our Children: Pre-school services in a changing society* (London, Temple Smith, 1976), p. 184.

35. Christopher Jencks, et al., *Inequality: A reassessment of the effect of family and schooling in America* (New York, Harper & Row, 1972, edition of 1973), p. 261.

36. Samuel Bowles and Herbert Gintis, *Schooling in Capitalist America: Educational reform and the contradictions of economic life* (London, Routledge and Kegan Paul, 1976), pp. 5-6, 18.

37. For a summary of the findings published between 1976 and 1978 see the Executive Summary, *The Compensatory Education Study*, July 1978, (Washington D.C.; National Institute of Education, 1978).

38. Barbara Heyns, *Summer Learning and the Effects of Schooling* (New York, Academic Press, 1978), pp. 9-10.

39. Christopher Jencks, foreward to Heyns, *Summer Learning*, and *Who Gets Ahead? The Determinants of Economic Success in America* (New York, Basic Books, 1979).

40. Irving Lazar, et al., *The Persistence of Preschool Effects: A long-term follow-up of fourteen infant and preschool experiments*, final report (U.S. Department of Health, Education and Welfare, September 1977).

41. Hodges, "The Worth of the Follow Through Experience."

42. *Educational Priority,* vol. 1, "EPA Problems and Policies;" vol. 3, "Curriculum Innovation in London's EPA's;" and vol. 4, "The West Riding Project," 1975.

43. A.H. Halsey, et al., *Origins and Destinations: Family, class, and education in modern Britain* (Oxford, Clarendon, 1980), p. 216.

44. Michael Rutter, et al., *15,000 Hours: Secondary schools and their effects on children* (London, Open Books, 1979).

45. A.H. Halsey, "Education Can Compensate," *New Society,* January 24, 1980; Bernstein, "Education Cannot Compensate for Society," *New Society,* February 26, 1970.

46. The Heritage Foundation, "Report of the Mandate for Leadership Project," mimeographed (Washington D.C., November 10, 1980), pp. 13, 30, 71.

47. Dan Finn, et al., "Social Democracy, Education and the Crisis," in *Working Papers in Cultural Studies 10, On Ideology* (Birmingham, England, Center for Contemporary Cultural Studies, 1977), pp. 147-8.

48. Bowles and Gintis, *Schooling in Capitalist America,* pp. 5, 13-14, 44, 240.

49. Martin Carnoy, "Is Compensatory Education Possible?," in Martin Carnoy and Henry Levin, eds., *The Limits of Educational Reform* (New York, David McKay, 1976), p. 216.

50. Henry M. Levin, "The Dilemma of Comprehensive Secondary School Reforms in Western Europe," *Comparative Education Review,* October 1978, p. 450.

MICHAEL F.D. YOUNG is the editor of *Knowledge and Control, Explorations in the Politics of School Knowledge,* and *Society, State and Schooling,* and the author of numerous articles in a wide variety of scholarly journals. He is a leading interpreter of the "new direction" sociology of education in Britain and currently is senior lecturer of sociology of education in the University of London.

Ideology and Educational Research

Michael F. D. Young

Although public education has come under increasing criticism both in the United States and the United Kingdom, and resources for curriculum development and educational research have been severely cut back, the widespread belief in the efficacy of "good" research has not been seriously questioned. Private foundations and state bodies continue to provide funds; university academics are encouraged to pursue research and are appointed, given tenure, and promoted on the basis of successful publication of their work; local educational authorities allow researchers into the schools they are responsible for and continue to grant study leave and financial assistance to teachers wishing to pursue research. Finally, a selection from the body of findings of educational research forms the basis of training courses for teachers and educational administrators, as well as being used to lend support to official policies and practices. Despite this investment and institutional support, most research never gets beyond the stage of the dissertation, the academic journal, or the training course reading list. Teachers remain skeptical:

Note: Some parts of this paper draw on an earlier paper of mine, "A Case Study of the Limitations of Policy Research," in Barbara Tizard, ed., *15,000 Hours: A Discussion* (London: University of London Institute of Education, 1980).

> ... returning to the university context (they) find themselves
> required to slog through a mass of research evidence and
> theory ... many come back in a state of confusion and with
> some considerable lack of confidence.[1]

Occasionally a piece of research transcends these narrow boundaries and generates a sense of authority, enthusiasm, and even outrage. It becomes, as was the case of the research reported in the book *15,000 Hours* by Michael Rutter and his colleagues, a media event.[2] I want to consider this case in some detail because I think it throws some light on educational research as a social institution and explains how it may be related to other features of contemporary education. In doing so, I hope to raise some questions about research as the basis of policy and practice and so to provide a more realistic guide to alternative forms of intervention in education. I shall start with the assumption that educational research, like other educational practice, is usefully viewed as one of the ways in which consent to an existing social order is maintained. This is not to say that educational research, any more than consent in general, goes unchallenged. In outlining his proposals for teacher-based action research, Jon Nixon recently argued that what was involved was "nothing short of a radical democratisation of the research community."[3]

In considering the study by Rutter and his colleagues, I want to examine that set of institutional practices that would have to be transformed for Nixon's proposal to become a reality. He suggests that this will only come about if "those who control the purse strings really want a thinking, questioning and enquiring force of teachers."[4]

It is my contention that, whatever their publicly avowed statements or intentions, those who fund and support educational research want no such thing, any more than managers *really* want thinking, questioning, inquiring workers. In other words, the democratization of educational research will not come about through the good offices of the Social Science Research Council or the National Institute of Education, regardless of the wishes of those involved. It will be part of a much wider and more complex political struggle over the control and content of education. Though educational research is at the periphery of this struggle both in resources and influence, in taking a case that in Britain became through the media a part of popular consciousness (albeit briefly), we may gain some understanding of the ideological forces at work, at least in education.

The remainder of this paper will have three parts:
I. Some preliminary comments on the concept of ideology.
II. Research methods as ideology—the *15,000 Hours* case.
III. Consequences and alternatives.

Ideology, Some Comments

In using the term ideology, I am not referring to false ideas but to a set of social practices through which partial views or accounts are presented as if they had some claim to universality. Typical examples are the ways public figures refer to "the national interest" or "the needs of industry." In this case I want to treat research findings in a similar way. They are produced as an abstraction from a complex context and then are generalized as a basis for policy and practice. This is not to reject generalizing but to recognize that generalizing is always to a purpose. We can go further with this notion of ideology through Marx's account of the production of commodities. Marx argues (and here I am following Robert Young in substituting scientific fact for commodity):

> A scientific fact appears, at first sight, a very trivial thing, and easily understood. Its analysis shows that it is, in reality, a very queer thing, abounding in metaphysical subtleties and theological niceties . . . A scientific fact is therefore a mysterious thing, simply because in it the social character of men's labour appears to them as an objective character stamped upon the product of that labour; because the relation of the producers to the sum total of their labour is presented to them as a social relation, existing not between themselves, but between the products of their labour, i.e., between scientific findings . . . A definite social relation between people assumes the fantastic form of a relation between things . . . This fetishism of scientific facts has its origin in the peculiar social character of the labour that produced them.[5]

To pick out one sentence, and recast it, ideology refers to the process in which "a definite social relation between people (researcher and researched) assumes the fantastic form of a relation between things (numbers). This fetishism . . . has its origins in the peculiar social character of the labour that produced [it]."

In education we are constantly confronted with things—curricular materials, educational technology, tests, timetables, scores, ranks, and gradings. We find them convenient, even necessary, in the contexts we find ourselves in. What Marx reminds us of is not the possiblity of a world in which no "things" exist, but that the things of our world are historical and changeable as "they bear it stamped upon them in unmistakeable letters that they belong to a state of society in which the process of production has control over men, instead of being controlled by them."[6]

In this paper I am concerned with educational research as a labor process, in which the "things" produced are findings or conclusions presented as facts, figures or, usually, probabilities. I am not concerned with the intentions of researchers, nor even of those who fund research (though neither are irrelevant) but with the social relations between those who carry out educational research and those—usually teachers and pupils—who are their objects. The ideological character of educational research is expressed through the way these social relations are part of the production but not of the form in which the product is presented. These social relations are directly opposite to those proposed by Jon Nixon and referred to earlier in the paper. They are asymmetric power relations, and they have a history that goes back to the establishment of the statistical societies in the nineteenth century. Such has been the ideological power of the methods of natural science as a mode of production of knowledge that in educational research, as in the other social sciences, researchers have rarely been challenged by the "objects" of research. The research community has been able to establish itself as largely autonomous from its resource—teachers and pupils— and thereby to gain not only public credibility but funding. It is not without significance that the dominant tradition of educational research has never conceived of investigations into the practices of the powerful. To return to the quotation from Marx, "the relation of producers [in this case teachers and pupils] is presented to them as a social relation, not between themselves, but between the products of their labour [achievement scores and teacher attributes, for example]." This is well exemplified in the following brief account of the Rutter research and its methods.

Research Methods as Ideology

Before considering the methods of the study *15,000 Hours*, I should like to indicate why it may be of specific significance to any consideration of ideology in education. First, it gained quite uncharacteristic media coverage in Britain; second, it quickly became the basis of new administrative procedures by secondary-school headteachers; third, despite appearing to support greater control over classroom teachers, it gained considerable plausibility among them; and fourth, the largely uncritical praise it received raises serious questions about the last ten years of social science in which the methodology of research of the kind used in this study has been under persistent attack. I will consider each of these points briefly in turn.

1. On publication, what were identified as the main findings of the study were reported on TV and radio and in the mass-circulation newpapers. This broad exposure highlights the way a research publication in the form of a book has to be viewed as a commodity that is sold on the market. This exposure was not only reflected in the publisher's promotional activities but also in the way the media's conception of the public view of education as a

consumption good influenced the findings that were given publicity (a parent's five-point check list for choosing "the best school for *your* child," as one newspaper put it).
2. Comments from teachers taking in-service courses have indicated that head teachers not merely welcomed the publication of *15,000 Hours* but used it as a basis for asserting greater administrative control over classroom teachers. This suggests a congruence between the social organization of research and the social organization of schools that I will return to.
3. In claiming to demonstrate conclusively that what teachers do in classrooms does influence pupil achievement, Michael Rutter and his colleagues evoked a sympathetic response from teachers uncharacteristic of much research of the last decade. They had been told that their achievements were largely due to luck (as Jencks would have it), to innate abilities (according to Jensen and his followers), or, as researchers both in the United Kingdom and the United States (such as Bowles and Gintis) have tried to demonstrate, to social class background or to the nature of capitalist society itself. Here at last was a study with all the characteristics of a scientific investigation that told teachers what they wanted to hear and seemed to offer them some support against the often overwhelming voice of their critics, both of the Right and the Left.
4. Although the findings of the Rutter study have been treated with some reservations in the academic journals, the prevailing acceptance of its methodology, which has undergone systematic and persistent criticism for more than a decade, suggests that the methodology itself has its basis not primarily in its credibility to the academic community but in the structure of the wider society. Before developing this point in relation to my earlier account of ideology, I shall turn now to a brief account of the method and model of research we find in the Rutter study.

Initially, the researchers were asked by those who funded them to identify the characteristics of a good school. So, certain general assumptions were built into the research from the beginning—namely, that such characteristics could be identified, with some claim to objectivity, which could be a basis for teachers in less successful schools to model their practice on. This point is made more explicit when we consider the researchers' method of interpreting the mass of data that they collected. In a way that is widespread in educational research, they divided the social world of the school into two kinds of relatively discrete sets of quantifiable variables. The dependent variables, or school outcomes, were those factors in the experience of pupils that are thought of as the outcome of going to school: attending regularly or not; good behavior or bad; doing well or badly academically; and committing or refraining from acts reported to and identified by the police as delinquent. The independent variables the researchers divided into four kinds: ecological; physical and administrative; intake factors; and school processes, which were themselves subdivided.

The basic unquestioned assumption of this variable analysis model of research is that the variables abstracted and their interrelatedness represent some kind of authoritative account. However, it does not take very much experience of schools at work to come up against all kinds of factors that such an abstraction or model leaves out. I am thinking of conflicts within the staff of a school over resources, timetable organization, teacher careers, sex and race divisions within the curriculum, and so forth. The question then becomes: Why is the particular reality abstracted in the variable analysis given primacy? It is, I suggest, because the researchers have a particular conception of what should count as an explanation of what goes on in schools; it involves being able, at least in principle, to predict and control outcomes—of input variables influencing outcomes—and therefore of a system that can be manipulated. As suggested earlier this conception of research has considerable affinity with an administrative view of schooling. By transposing the research model of the laboratory, in which variables are interpreted from the dead material world and are given meaning in their manipulation, the actions of teachers and pupils have become transformed by educational researchers into variables or things. This then is the concrete expression of the points I raised at the beginning of this paper about ideology as a social process. The products of the social relations between researchers and the researched—interview, observation, filling in and coding a questionnaire—become things, abstracted from the conflicting interests and purposes in which they were generated. There are two senses in which the relations are ones of unequal distribution of power. First, it is the teachers and pupils who have to fit into the schedules, choices, and priorities of the researchers. Second, the strategies of resistance that the researched can always adopt (researchers never know whether their respondents are playing safe, playing for a laugh, or whatever) never become available in the final accounts presented as findings. This again serves to emphasize the administrative conception of the research. In ranking different schools in their proportion of "well behaving pupils," no insights are given to the teachers as to *why* pupils engage in various actions interpreted by the researchers as bad behavior; arriving late, chewing gum, or combing hair are indices of "bad" behavior, but are available only for correlation, not for understanding.

Other examples of the way this model of variable analysis, with its notion of prediction and control, is linked to particular concepts of administrative practice are worth citing. Teacher punctuality and regular marking of books were picked out in the media and by head teachers from among the variables that showed a statistically significant correlation with pupil achievement. Thus science, in the form of research findings, was drawn on to support more centralized control of classroom teachers. We have, then, a kind of managerial practice set in the language of science that excludes culture, meaning, and history. The ideological character of research within this tradition is not primarily at the level of the findings or even how they are used, though neither factor is irrelevant; it is rather at the level of method. Let me illustrate:

As in any research, selection was unavoidable. In this case the researchers chose twelve schools on which they had prior data on the pupils, so that their study could be longitudinal. The likelihood of ecological or sociostructural factors being significant was minimized by the relative homogeneity of the area in which the schools were located. It does not require any imputing of intentions to the researchers to recognize that the research fitted neatly into a climate of cuts in public expenditure on education. In effect, though not directly, by a focus on intraschool processes, the message of the research was that rather than expanding resources, improving staff/pupil ratios, and building new schools, schools can improve if teachers work harder and are more punctual. In other words, a study that puts great emphasis on what teachers can do to improve school outcomes, and backs its claims with the legitimacy and objectivity of statistical analyses, necessarily deemphasizes other elements in the complex totality of school-society relations. In *15,000 Hours* teachers are viewed, as they tend to see themselves, as able to influence what goes on in the school and classroom, but as able to do little about those matters that mediate society in the school. Not surprisingly, therefore, such matters take on a hazy and diffuse reality. Social-class relations are not mentioned, inequalities are expressed as differences in social background, the hierarchy of occupations in the division of labor is reduced to differences of ability and balance of intake and is totally neglected in terms of how it acts on the academic/nonacademic divisions in the curriculum.

The ideological work of such research is accomplished by the way it abstracts schools and teachers from the complexities of the society and then puts responsibility on them for changing a situation that is only in a limited way in their power. Such research provides no way for teachers to understand the nature of the constraints on them, let alone to develop alternative strategies.

I have placed considerable emphasis on the method rather than on the findings of research. It follows, therefore, that even if such research had come up with quite opposite findings—for instance, that pupil achievement was associated with resources and staff-pupil ratios rather than with teacher attitudes and punctuality—the critique of it as ideological practice would still follow; the research would still be congruent with particular power relations in the distribution of resources, though it might well bring the contradictions in these relations to the fore.

Consequences and Alternatives

What are the alternatives? First, the research tradition of ethnographic work associated with educational anthropology and interpretive sociology remains important in its capacity to capture something of the culture and texture of school life. It offers a kind of generalization and objectivity associated with the way those not part of the context of the research can identify with the accounts that are created. However, ethnographic studies themselves are also ideological; they express power relations between researchers and researched and are limited to descriptions of the multiple realities of the school within the context in which they are located. They cannot explore the mediation of power relations of the wider society in curricula and pedagogy, as they lack an overall perspective on how to set the conflicts within the school within any wider structure of conflict. Research cannot escape the prevailing power relations any more than it can find some ideology-free approach or method. Research has its history in a scientific tradition that claimed to free people from past traditions and dogmas. In practice, by neglecting its own power relations as well as those it studies, research becomes little more than another mode of social control.

Research initiated by teachers (or pupils) would not itself escape the kind of analysis developed here, though it would express different demands and purposes, and generate different methodologies related to those purposes. In bringing out the competing purposes of research it would make educational research more explicitly a part of political debates and struggles.

Because the structures of schooling appear so fixed and bounded, educational research has to be historical. Research can attempt to show how the living labor of the past is present in the curriculum packages and texts of today. It has to make questions of the content and control of education public issues, not issues of technical or professional competence, in which research hides its social character in numbers or jargon.

The kind of educational research I am describing can display the real relations that are masked in the structures of schooling, but it must also be able to point to possibilities—to display in practice the involvement and excitement of learning and teaching that would be politically subversive if it was not so rare. The purpose of analyzing research as ideology is to suggest that it is yet another arena in which struggles, conflicts, and opposition are played out and that such struggles carry elements of the contest over the social division of labor and the appropriation of the value of that labor, which are manifested in different ways in quite other contexts. In that sense educational research serves to emphasize the need to conceive of any educational practice in terms of the structures of reproduction as well as of the struggles to oppose such structures.

FOOTNOTES

1. Letter to the editor, *Times Educational Supplement,* June 5, 1981.

2. Michael Rutter, et al., *15,000 Hours: Secondary Schools and Their Effect on Children* (London, Open Books; 1979).

3. Jon Nixon, "A Teacherly Perspective," *Times Educational Supplement,* May 15, 1981.

4. Ibid.

5. Robert Young, "Science *is* Social Relations," *Radical Science Journal,* 5, 1977, quoting K. Marx, *Capital,* Vol. 1 (London; Lawrence and Wishart, 1970), p. 71.

6. Ibid., p. 80.

EDGAR Z. FRIEDENBERG is author of *The Vanishing Adolescent, Coming of Age in America, The Dignity of Youth and Other Atavisms, R. D. Laing, The Disposal of Liberty and Other Industrial Wastes, Deference to Authority: The Case of Canada,* and other books. He is a distinguished critic, and his essays have been published by *Commentary, Dissent, New York Review of Books, Harper's,* and a wide variety of professional journals. Dr. Friedenberg has taught at the University of Chicago, City University of New York, the University of California, and the State University of New York at Buffalo. He is currently a professor of education at Dalhousie University in Halifax, Nova Scotia.

Deference to Authority: Education in Canada and the United States

Edgar Z. Friedenberg

In folklore and in fact, schools and authority go together like law 'n order and ham 'n eggs. The school, the police station, and the prison are the last strongholds of the cruder forms of authority; in North America, only the school retains the right to beat people who disobey its rules, though in practice, police and prison guards may do so with impunity. Though an alleged wide-spread decline in academic standards is often publicly deplored, lack of discipline in the schools is regarded as a more serious problem and one which arouses more acrimony.

Meanwhile, school discipline has become less harsh through the years, though teachers' associations still lobby for the right to beat children when they deem this necessary for the preservation of order. They use, or abuse, the right less often now, but what is important is that they think such a right exists, and that order is what it preserves. Methods of enforcement change with fashions in social character, but the concept of the school as a basically coercive institution does not.

Authority is indeed the complex core issue that complicates the theory and practice of education. The word *authority* refers to a variety of quite distinct social and philosophical functions, each of which is not only relevant but problematic to education. What I hope to do in this paper is to show how these different aspects of authority affect education and, especially, schooling in ways both complementary and contrasting.

It is helpful to start with the distinction Erich Fromm made so familiar, between *rational* and *irrational* authority. By *rational* authority, Fromm meant authority derived from competence, experience, and expertise. Recognition and acceptance of such authority and a willingness to defer to it within its legitimate limits is seen as a mark of realism and personal maturity, of freedom from the need to rebel without a cause. The pilot flies the plane; he has been trained to do so, and passengers who attempt by coercive means to usurp his function and alter his destination are decried as tasteless and impulsive, not hailed as enterprising and creative.

The converse form of authority, *irrational authority*, is derived from the power to threaten and punish and, especially, to invoke the latent fears and anxieties each of us retains from the unresolved conflicts and the smarting defeats of childhood, which keep us from realizing the competencies we posess and could develop and induce us to submit to the will of other people and acknowledge their right to rule us. Such authority is denoted by badges of rank and status that, in a secular society, are supposed to correspond to differences in competence: hence, licensing laws and academic and professional degrees. There is a relationship between competence and status, though not a very dependable one; but the significance of this relationship is overshadowed by the fact that one is not permitted to gain the status and the authority the relationship legitimates by demonstrating the competence without going through channels. Every few years the same corny story pops up in a different locale, about some dedicated soul who has zealously tended the maimed and ailing in an isolated community for 25 years, earning the devotion of its people, when he is revealed by some misfortune unrelated to his skill not to be a doctor at all—he never got his license, or the medical society back in the capital disbarred him 30 years ago for excessive gynecological zeal, or something. So off he goes to prison, the town is left without medical care, though the state stops short of declaring his former patients legally dead of neglect, as it ought logically to do. In a conflict between irrational authority and rational authority, irrational authority usually wins, precisely because it does derive from immediate or potential coercive power.

One is tempted to simplify by holding, as Fromm did, that irrational authority is the *bad* kind and rational authority the *good* kind; and in terms of human growth this is true. The exercise and acceptance of rational authority increases our competence and our awareness and acceptance of our own limits; it makes us more trustworthy and better-centered. Irrational authority stunts the growth and development both of those who submit to it and those who wield it, leaving them hung-up and crippled by existential guilt. Tyrants and devils end up frozen in their own excrement. The metaphor, timeless in every way, is Dante's. Moreover, the kind of authority we usually associate with school *is irrational* authority. Without exercising irrational authority vigorously and continuously, school would not keep for a day. The practice and the folklore of teaching abound with devices for showing pupils from the first minute who is in charge, not letting them think they can get away with anything. The teacher should have eyes in the back of her head and never smile before Christmas, coming, in the process one supposes, to resemble one of Picasso's less amiable drawings. Contemporary schools, especially in middle-class neighborhoods, put a much better face on things as well as on teachers, but as long as schools depend on compulsory attendance, coercion remains the bottom line, though the cane may no longer be used for its inscription. As Paul Willis puts it in *Learning to Labour:*

> Discipline becomes a matter not of punishment for wrongs committed in the old testament sense, but of maintaining the institutional axis, of reproducing the social relationships of school in general: of inducing respect for elemental frameworks in which other transactions can take place . . . It is the moral intensity of maintaining this axis and attempting to exclude or suppress the contradictory, murky cross-currents of normal life which can give to the school a cloying, claustrophobic feel of arrested adolescence . . . In this sense the school is a kind of totalitarian regime. There is relatively little direct coercion or oppression, but an enormous constriction of the range of moral possibilities. Everything is neatly tied in, every story has the same ending, every analogy has the same analogue.[1]

This passage of Willis', condensed and in some ways obscure as it is, is the heart of a most illuminating essay on education. For, in the course of its development, Willis suggests very strongly to the reader that the authority schools seek to establish over pupils is not merely irrational but suprarational; it glides smugly above the field of daily experience, immune to the challenge of either passion or empirical experience:

> The school is the agency of face-to-face control *par excellence*. The stern look of the enquiring teacher; the relentless pursuit of 'the truth' set up as a value even above good behaviour; the common weapon of ridicule; the techniques learned over time whereby particular troublemakers can 'always be reduced to tears;' the stereotyped deputy head, body poised, head lowered, finger jabbing the culprit; the head unexpectedly bearing down on a group in the corridor—these are all tactics

for exposing and destroying, or freezing, the private. What successful conventional teaching cannot tolerate is private reservation, and in the early forms in virtually any school it is plain to see that most kids yield that capacity willingly. The eager first form hands reaching and snapping to answer first are all seeking approval from an acknowledged superior in a very particular institutional form. And in the individual competition for approval the possibility of any private reservations becoming shared to form any oppositional definition of the situation is decisively controlled. . .

In a simple physical sense school students, and their possible views of the pedagogic situation, are subordinated by the constricted and inferior space they occupy. Sitting in tight ranked desks in front of the larger teacher's desk; deprived of private space themselves but outside nervously knocking on the forbidden staff room door or the headmaster's door with its foreign rolling country beyond; surrounded by locked up or out-of-bounds rooms, gyms and equipment cupboards; cleared out of school at break with no quarter given even in the unprivate toilets; told to walk at least two feet from staff cars in the drive—all of these things help to determine a certain orientation to the physical environment and behind that to a certain kind of social organization. They speak to the whole *position* of the student. . .

Perhaps the classic move here, and one which is absolutely typical of the old secondary modern school and still widespread in working class comprehensives, is the revision from an objective to a moral basis of what is in the teacher's gift and is to be exchanged by him for obedience, politeness and respect from students. . . . . The importance of all this is not, of course, that the values and stances involved might be admirable or execrable, correct or incorrect, or whatever. The point is a formal one: the moral term, unlike the objective one, is capable of infinite extension and assimilation because it has no real existence except in itself. The real world cannot act as a court of appeal. Moral definitions make their own momentum. So far as the basic teaching paradigm is concerned what it is worth the student striving for becomes, not knowledge and the promise of qualification, but somehow deference and politeness themselves . . . The pivotal notion of 'attitudes' and particularly of 'right attitudes' makes its entry here. Its presence should always warn us of a mystificatory transmutation of basic exchange relationships into illusory, ideal ones. If one approaches school and its authority, it seems, 'with the right attitude' then employers and work will also be approached with the 'right attitude' in such a way indeed that real social and economic advances can be made—all without the help of academic achievement or success. Of course this crucial move renders the basic paradigm strictly circular and tautological since the same thing is being offered on both sides . . . What the student gets all around is deference and subordination to authority. He could learn this for himself."[2]

So one might easily proceed on the assumption that the oppressive and constrictive aspects of school, pervasive as they are, are chiefly expressions of irrational authority—which is true—and hence conclude that, to the degree that this can be replaced by rational authority, schooling would become more liberating—which, I fear, is untrue. Irrational authority is poisonous; but rational authority is like medicine; helpful when you need it, but even then you have to watch for the side effects, and most of the time we stay healthier without taking anything at all—off anybody. Even the best medicine is toxic in overdose, or if taken at the wrong time. So is rational authority, especially in the school context.

Rational authority is no cure-all, the concept is fraught with treacherous ambiguity. Fromm's distinction between rational and irrational authority now seems culture-bound, as, in fact, it clearly was when he made it. Only a bourgeois social-democrat could hold to this distinction for long. The chief source of the difficulty is the ideological character of the concept of rationality itself. To be recognized as rational in our culture, authority must be orderly and dispassionate, objective and evenhanded, blind to poetic insight, and immune to the influence of the flashes of insight each of us finds more convincing than any other evidence when we experience them personally, but which we long ago learned better than to try to share with others.

Rational authority, then, lacks some of the components that are quite generally recognized as essential to the formation of policy and the conduct of life. But these deficiencies tend to be reduced by common sense and the cake of custom, which includes the irrational factors needed for survival, often in quantities greatly in excess of our minimum daily requirements. This does not happen, however, in the processes by which knowledge becomes formally defined as authoritative in the school curriculum. As an example of what *does* happen, may I remind you of the ghastly lecture on sex education provided to a segregated audience of adolescent boys in Northeast High School, Philadelphia, by a physician in Frederick Wiseman's classic film *High School*. The doctor reduces sexuality—limited, of course, to conventional heterosexuality—to a mechanical process having nothing to do with personal feeling or commitment, though he defers to established cultural convention by treating the process as a dirty joke on girls. This, I would suggest, is a much more serious impediment to the development of real intimacy between lovers than the hellfire sermon that so shakes turn of the century Irish schoolboys in *Portrait of the Artist as a Young Man*, which at least insisted that passion has serious personal consequences both in this world and the next, while leaving the more mature and self-confident students consolingly though secretly aware that they knew more about the subject from personal experience than their mentor could claim. The priest, in his sermon, asserted a fiercely threatening and totally irrational authority. He did not, however, present himself as a qualified expert on sex; only on sin, which the sciences, in their pretense of ethical neutrality, define as an area beyond their competence or understanding.

In its own peculiar way, rational authority in our sort of culture becomes as factitious, coercive, and bloody as irrational authority, while remaining in every sense of the word less engaging. The difficulty, or one way of putting it, is that rational authority has come to be almost synonymous with technical expertise and is seen as concerned solely with means—not with ends, which the means tend to generate. Once nuclear energy becomes technically possible it has to be utilized, while the scientific mentality that made it possible declares itself incompetent to deal with the value judgments by which the decision must be made. But nuclear energy does not just *become* possible; it is made possible by a whole series of prior policy decisions as to what research is to be done, by whom, and under what conditions of sponsorship, access, and control. These decisions and the processes by which they are reached might themselves be the objects of rational investigation by political scientists, economists, and sociologists, but are effectively shielded by involving the needs of national security or simply by denying outsiders access to documents or the opportunity to observe. Meanwhile, our sometimes crude but shrewd insights into how these things are accomplished, based on normal political savvy and a sense of *cui bono,* are less persuasive, though in fact no less rational, than they would have been in a society less impressed by the canons of scientific proof. So are our moral convictions.

It was not always thus. Teleology, "the study of evidences of design and purpose in nature," and axiology, "the branch of philosophy dealing with values, as those of ethics, aesthetics or religion"—both definitions are from the Random House unabridged dictionary—are rational disciplines, and competently applied they become sources of wisdom. This does not, of course, mean that academic study in these areas is likely to turn graduates into philosopher-kings any more than the study of medicine turns all licensed physicians into healers. But, today, teleological reasoning is dismissed as irrational and superstitious per se; though those who dwell on the banks of the Love Canal may have reason to wonder whether nature is cross with the Happy Hooker and venting her wrath on them. Certainly, without some sense of teleology, it is difficult to take seriously the notion that nature may be subject to violation, as often we have seen it done and as serious as the consequences have clearly become.

Teleological and axiological thought, however rational, cannot be scientific and, for that reason, can no longer claim or even contribute much to rational authority. This development has some curious consequences. It is quite true that one cannot prove, in the scientific sense, the validity of a moral or aesthetic judgment, or establish by controlled observation and path-analysis the inscrutable purposes of nature. But rational authority need not rest on either proof or faith. Trust is different from either of these; it is, or certainly had better be, empirically based, in that we feel it and establish its limits in response to our unique experiences of other persons and of ourselves. The judgments involved are rational but subjective; they are derived from genuine though sometimes subliminal perceptions that cannot, by their nature, be replicated. It is useful, if one is not to make a real mess of life, to learn to trust such judgments, favorable or adverse as the case may be, as well as to remember, as Cromwell beseeched, that we may be mistaken.

Rational authority reduced to the habit of deference to technical expertise cannot be trusted. In its own field, technical expertise is certainly superior to irrational authority; without it, irrational authority cannot make the trains run on time or keep the airports open or bug the enemies' phones. But rational authority castrated, deprived of the power to inform moral judgments, cannot effectively contend with irrational authority; it can only lend its skills to dirty business that it has agreed it has no special competence to challenge. Which notoriously, is what usually occurs.

What has schooling to do with all this?

The function of schooling is essentially hegemonic. Antonio Gramsci's now familiar concept of hegemony really embraces all the school's essential activities, and provides the most useful conceptual tool for understanding what schools do; and why, as they approach industrial development, all states feel they have to install schools and compel their youth to attend them; and why, despite extreme differences in socio-economic systems, schools are so very much alike. In this respect, Urie Bronfenbrenner's classic *Two Worlds of Childhood: U.S. and U.S.S.R.* is a very scary piece of work.[3] Schooling is ubiquitous as well as egregious; there is just no way to get away from it. Schools in space will doubtless soon be administered by joint Soviet-American committees without much tendency to find themselves working at cross-purposes.

Toward the middle of the nineteenth century when state-supported schools were just getting established (long before Gramsci was recognized by the Italian government of Benito Mussolini and provided with the means and the privacy to develop his theoretical position), the hegemonic function of the school was regarded as self-evident, though the term hegemony was not used.

Daniel Webster and Horace Mann, in the United States, and Egerton Ryerson, who founded the Ontario school system before Canada became a nation (if, indeed, it ever has), argued that schooling would establish a benign and internalized self-policing force in the minds of the otherwise potentially rebellious poor, nipping any possible revolutionary tendencies in the bud. In England, in 1846, in a letter to Lord John Russell urging the establishment of a school system, one E. Baines "suggested that 'a system of state education is a vast intellectual police force, set to watch over the young . . . to prevent the intrusion of dangerous thoughts and turn their minds into safe channels'."[4] Webster and Ryerson, too, explicitly used the word "police" to characterize the utility of a public school system.

There was no "hidden curriculum" in those days, when the authority associated with social stratification was explicit. Indeed, there is social progress, at least in the short run. Leonard L. Richards, in his fascinating 1970 study of pro-slavery mob violence in the United States in the 1830s, had no methodological difficulties in justifying his sardonic title *Gentlemen of Property and Standing*.[5] It is taken from one of the contemporary accounts in local newspapers that, as if reporting who was present and having a ball, identified the solid citizens who had proudly assisted in these macabre events. Today, oppression in North America takes subtler and less candid forms. If the basic social functions of schooling remain much what they were, the process is more oblique. School personnel share the liberal ideology of the times, often much more fully than their lower-status pupils. They, even more than their students, must be mystified by the routines, and the routinized assumptions, of the institution in which they serve. If they understood what they were doing, they couldn't really bear to go on doing it. Hence hegemony.

Hegemony is more than, and different from, propaganda or brainwashing, though these may play a part in maintaining it. Usually, nothing so assertive is implied. Hegemony is established through the operation of the entire set of assumptions, conventions, values, and categories of thought and feeling that are validated by a society and serve to legitimate and protect its dominant institutions and elites from being examined critically on terms other than their own; or more precisely, from "the intrusion of dangerous thoughts," or the turning of the mind into unsafe channels.

The effects of hegemony, like those of a specialized lens, vary with the object in view. It sharpens attention to and sometimes perception of messages that are useful in keeping the existing social apparatus on course. It reinterprets discordant messages so that they may be assimilated into established presuppositions with minimum conflict. But it distorts or filters perceptions that threaten the established order, or the established system of disorder, thus hastening the demise of those who, when some novel emergency arises, stand in critical need of timely warning. Hegemony makes it unnecessary to kill the messenger who bears illtidings; it insures that he will not be listened to, like Cassandra, or misunderstood until too late, like the Delphic oracle. Hegemony is nothing new.

Nor is there anything new about a society depending on a universal and official institution to establish and propagate acceptable ways of looking at the world. In the West the church has served the purposes of hegemony for millennia while traditional societies, almost by definition, are much more completely hung-up on their own mythos and ethos than are modern ones. Indeed, the distinctive feature of modern societies has been their ingenuity in channeling new insights into technological development without suggesting that the same flexibility of mind might be used to challenge the legitimacy of the social order itself, and the moral assumptions it rests on. Without some such guarantee of extraterritorial immunity for the sacred and the powerful, innovation is scarcely tolerable; and, in most of the world most of the time, there hasn't been much.

We have several notable institutions that serve in this way as semiconductors of insight. The scientific method, as vulgarly conceived with its startling presumption of ethical neutrality, is one. The school system is another. The rise of the democratic, industrial state—a polity that renews its legitimacy by the ceremonial evocation of formal popular consent—requires that hegemony be justified as service. Or, as I put it—rather more simply—on an earlier occasion, "The school, as a social institution, developed as the adjunct of industrialism . . . precisely because a rapidly expanding technology of production and administration promised a world that seemed so various, so beautiful, so new that mighty new inhibitions were required to keep pace with the new seductions . . . If you want progress on a large scale, you must have schooling to keep people from taking advantage of it."[6] Thus, it should be noted that one of the casualties of the hegemonic process, and especially of centering that process in an educational system supposedly obligated to follow truth wherever it may lead, is the cherished distinction between rational and irrational authority. For even rational authority, to which a free man owes honorable deference, turns out to be so limited by what the schools make of it that it can neither be tested by common sense—"the real world cannot act as a court of appeal" against what is taught in school, as Willis observed—nor serve as a source of genuinely subversive or liberating insights.

Hegemony comes first, and what it supports is neither rational authority nor irrational authority, but just authority itself. How is this done? Within the past decade, educational research has provided a small fortune for the ethnographic study of schools that helps us to answer this question with a feeling of somewhat greater certainty than we could previously have done. There is, admittedly, a certain irony in this observation, which becomes a further tribute to our obeisance to scientific, as opposed to common-sense, knowledge. Probably everyone in this room with the exception of myself has attended grade school or high school, or even both: so you have all done your own field work. True, things change: methods, techniques, equipment, modes of organization—even the social function of education changes somewhat as society itself does, creating a market for different personality-types and life-styles. But Willard Waller wrote his classic, *The Sociology of Teaching* fifty years ago—Wiley published it in 1932, while Herbert Hoover was still in office—and it adumbrates nearly everything of importance we have learned since about how schools work; though its author, who simply told it as he knew it to be, without benefit of formal data, remained academically marginal for the rest of his life.

Formal research in education continued to develop as essentially black-box research concerned with the improvement of in-house procedures. There was not much observation of what actually went on from day-to-day in schools. Studies of social-class bias in the educative process became and remained conventional from the late 1930s on; but for the most part these dealt with structural questions like the social composition of school boards, or factors associated with differences in achievement in schools having differing demographic characteristics. James Coleman's government-sponsored grandfalon, *Equality of Educational Opportunity,* published in 1966, went about as far in this direction as you can go; and Coleman has since retracted most of it. Meanwhile, ethnographic research in American education developed, almost incidentally, as a part of Lloyd Warner's new—in the 1930s—anthropological study of American communities. Having begun like any normal anthropologist of the day by studying Australian aborigines, Warner took the giant step of turning his attention to the study of folkways in small cities of his own land. In his landmark *Yankee City* studies of Newburyport, Massachusetts, the schools hardly figured. But when Warner turned his attention to the American middle west in *Democracy in Jonesville,* and when August Hollingshead did his spin-off study of the same population, *Elmtown's Youth* (Wiley, 1949), the high school, at least, emerged as the central institution it was (and is) in midwestern small-town life. (Warner and his colleagues on *Jonesville* had, in fact, developed a specialized interest in the role of the schools in perpetuating social stratification, and had already published, in 1944, *Who Shall Be Educated?*) Highly regarded as a radical critique of the role of school in society at the time, Hollingshead's work was, anthropologically speaking, a retrograde step away from sharp ethnographic observation and toward polemic based on demographic social-class data. Even the Yankee City work had depended heavily on, and been distinguished by, the use of quasi-quantitative methods of codifying and analyzing observations, like the Index of Status Characteristics and the more subjective Index of Evaluated Participation, that went far to make the work seem acceptably hard science even as they dulled its vividness.

Anthropology, too, claims to be value-free and thus respectably scientific. But this claim is much more effective in shielding an outlandish tribe from the ethical judgments of visiting cosmopolitan observers than it can be when observer and observed share the same culture. When Hollingshead notes in *Elmstown's Youth* that
"the administration of discipline laid bare the dynamics of the class system in a way that is directly observable but difficult to quantify. We were in an advantageous position to see the school as it was administered from the principal's office because we sat in one corner of the office to do our formal interviewing. In the course of the year, the principal, teachers, and students became so accustomed to us that they came and went about their business seemingly oblivious to our presence. From this vantage point, we watched the school function and attempted to comprehend some of what we saw."[7]

We recognize and, if so inclined, admire his devotion to scientific rigor. But when he continues by observing the principal, in the presence of the superintendent of schools, slapping around a student the principal has previously described by saying, "His old man is a laborer out at the fertilizer plant and the kid thinks he's someone, humph!" pulling the boy's cap down over his eyes and hitting "him three times with the heel of his hand on the back of the neck near the base of the skull," we cannot, much as we may admire Hollingshead's remarkable *sangfroid,* dismiss the matter as an example of the quaint customs of the people of Morris, Illinois. It hits home.

Mainstream anthropology was again, however, to seize the initiative from sociology and the discipline of education itself as observer of the actual processes of schooling in Jules Henry's remarkable observations in the "Golden Rule Days: American Classrooms" and "Rome High School" sections of *Culture Against Man.*[8] Unlike Warner, Henry never developed a specialized interest in schooling or in social stratification as such. What concerned him was the unplanned but systematic development of social institutions that alienate people from one another and themselves in the interests of fitting them for the demands of modern society. Henry did not merely sit in classrooms and observe what went on; he lived as a friendly boarder in the homes of families that were driving their children mad; and these experiences, too, are related in *Culture Against Man*. But for children whose parents are unwilling or unable to perform this service, schools are the next most powerful available resource. Henry's observations of the development of competition and patterns of mutual denigration among pupils learning to seek the teacher's attention by giving right answers to meaningless or irrelevant questions, and of high school students rating and dating (thirty years after Waller had coined the phrase to describe the practice), are unforgettable.

Before Jules Henry died in 1968, he had begun a study that Ray C. Rist, also then at Washington University, St. Louis, was to complete and publish in 1970 as "Student Social Class and Teacher Expectations: The Self-Fulfilling Prophecy in Ghetto Education."[9] The term landmark study is overused, but this really is one; not because its findings are astonishing, but because its simple and impeccable methodology makes them unanswerable.

Henry, Rist, and their co-workers followed the members of a St. Louis kindergarten class who continued to attend school in the same building through the second grade. All administrators, teachers, staff, and pupils in the school during the study were black, so the crude factor of racial discrimination is not involved in what went on in the school, though its antecedent effects on all the actors in this situation certainly were. As to the possibility that this school was an unusually bad example of its kind, Rist notes that

> the school in which this study occurred was selected by the District Superintendent as one of five available to the research team. All five schools were visited during the course of the study and detailed observations were conducted in four of them. The principal of the school reported upon in this study commented that I was very fortunate in coming to his school since his staff (and the kindergarten teacher in particular) were equal to "any in the city."[10]

At the time of the study, the building was less than ten years old.

For the pupils in this school, the kindergarten teacher was important. She was about as important as God, if not quite as quick; it took her eight days to create the world the children would live in for the rest of their academic lives and, to some degree, their whole lives. On the eighth day of school, she gave the children permanent seating assignments at one of three tables; and thereafter justified the basis for the assignment in terms of the children's ability. Table

1 was made up of "fast learners"; Table 3 of children who "just had no idea of what was going on in the classroom." But, in fact, she had no information about these children's ability, only about their social class characteristics. There were no aptitude test data, for example, but there was information

> supplied two days before the beginning of school by the school social worker who provided a tentative list of all children enrolled in the kindergarten who lived in homes that received public welfare funds. . . . It should be noted that not one of those four sources of information to the teacher was related directly to the academic potential of the incoming kindergarten child. Rather, they concerned various types of social information revealing such facts as the financial status of certain families, medical care of the child, presence or absence of a telephone in the home, as well as the structure of the family in which the child lived, i.e., number of siblings, whether the child lived with both, one, or neither of his natural parents.[11]

Of course, an experienced teacher can learn a lot about a child in eight school days. But *learning ability?* Here is one of Mrs. Caplow's lessons:

> (The students are involved in acting out a skit arranged by the teacher on how a family should come together to eat the evening meal.) The students acting the roles of mother, father, and daughter are all from Table 1. The boy playing the son is from Table 2. At the small dinner table set up in the centre of the classroom, the four children are supposed to be sharing with each other what they had done during the day—the father at work, the mother at home, and the two children at school. The Table 2 boy makes few comments. (In real life he has no father and his mother is supported by ADC funds.) The teacher comments, 'I think we are going to have to let Milt (Table 1) be the new son, Sam, why don't you go and sit down. Milt, you seem to be the one who would know what a son is supposed to do at the dinner table. You come and take Sam's place.[12]

As Rist observes, with perhaps a hint of dryness, in his statement on methodology, "the utilization of longitudinal study as a research method in a ghetto school will enhance the possibilities of gaining further insight into mechanism of adaptation utilized by black youth to what appears to be a basically white, middle-class, value oriented institution."

Though no white folks except Rist were present, you better believe it. Before these children have passed out of Mrs. Caplow's hands she has reduced them, by a combination of selective inattention and sugary insult, to a condition where the Table 1 students do all the talking, much of it directed as derogatory comment at the students at Tables 2 and 3 for being stupid and dirty. They do not, however, attack one another. But the children at Tables 2 and 3 do, calling each other "dumb-dumb," "nigger," and "almondhead." When necessary, Mrs. Caplow reinforces these lessons:

> The children were preparing to go on a field trip to a local dairy. The teacher has designated Gregory (Table 1) as the 'sheriff' for the trip. . . . Mrs. Caplow simply watched as Gregory would walk up to a student and push him back into line saying, 'Boy, stand where you suppose to.' Several times he went up to students from Table 3, showed them the badge that the teacher had given to him and said, "Teacher made me Sheriff."[13]

That's hegemony; and an interesting choice of role-model for a black teacher to impose on black children in a border city in the late 1960s. Yet, sad as it is, this too shall pass. But it didn't.

The first grade teacher also used a three-table seat assignment; and she, of course, did have the record of the kindergarten year to go on. "Those children whom she placed at 'Table A' had all been Table 1 students in kindergarten." No student who had sat at Table 2 or 3 in kindergarten was placed at Table A in the first grade. Instead, all the students from Table 2 and 3—with one exception— were placed together at Table B. Table C was reserved for the first-grade teacher's own failures—grade repeaters—and for one girl from Mrs. Caplow's Table 3 whose low self-esteem had left her almost psychotic.

Precisely the same process continues thereafter:

> Of the original thirty students in kindergarten and eighteen in first grade, ten students were assigned to the only second grade class in the main building. . . . The teacher in the second grade also divided the class into three groups, though she did not give them number or letter designations. Rather, she called the first group the "Tigers." The middle group she labeled the "Cardinals," while the second-grade repeaters plus several new children assigned to the third table were designated by the teacher as "Clowns." . . . In the second-grade seating scheme, no student from the first grade who had not sat at Table A was moved "up" to the Tigers at the beginning of the second grade. All those students who in first grade had been at Table B or Table C and returned to second grade were placed in the Cardinal group. The Clowns consisted of six second-grade repeaters plus three students who were new to the class. . . .
>
> By the time the children came to the second grade, their seating arrangement appeared to be based not on the teacher's expectations of how the child might perform, but rather on the basis of past performance of the child. Available to the teacher when she formulated the seating groups were grade sheets from both kindergarten and first grade, IQ scores from kindergarten, listing of parental occupations for approximately half the class, reading scores from a test given to all students at the end of first grade, evaluations from the speech teacher and also the informal evaluations from both the kindergarten and first-grade teachers.

> The most important data utilized by the teacher in devising seating groups were the reading scores indicating the performance of the students at the end of the first grade. The second-grade teacher indicated that she attempted to divide the groups primarily on the basis of these scores. . . . The caste character of the reading groups became clear as the year progressed, in that all three groups were reading in different books and it was school policy that no child could go on to a new book until the previous one had been completed. Thus there was no way for the child, should he have demonstrated competence at a higher reading level, to advance, since he had to continue at the pace of the rest of his reading group. The teacher never allowed individual reading in order that a child might finish a book on his own and move ahead. *No matter how well a child in the lower reading groups might have read, he was destined to remain in the same reading group.* [italics Rist's]. . . Initial expectations of the kindergarten teacher two years earlier as to the ability of the child resulted in placement in a reading group, whether high or low, from which there appeared to be no escape. The child's journey through the early grades of school at one reading level and in one social grouping appeared to be preordained from the eighth day of kindergarten.[14]

Kindergarten, however, lays the foundations of hegemony in ways more directly ideological than by the reification of the social-class framework. Michael W. Apple, with Nancy King, in the third chapter of his original and insightful *Ideology and Curriculum* superbly details the process of socialization in kindergarten: "learning of norms and definitions of social interactions." In the kindergarten it was observed:

> . . . the children had no part in organizing the classroom materials and were relatively impotent to affect the course of daily events. . . . The objects in the classroom were attractively displayed in an apparent invitation for the class to interact with them. Most of the materials were placed on the floor or on shelves within easy reach of the children. However, the opportunities to interact with materials in the classroom were severely circumscribed. The teacher's organization of time in the classroom contradicted the apparent availability of materials in the physical setting. During most of the kindergarten session, the children were not permitted to handle objects. The materials, then, were organized so that the children learned restraint; they learned to handle things within easy reach only when permitted to do so by the teacher. . . . For example, the teacher praised the children for their prompt obedience when, being told to do so, they quickly stopped bouncing basketballs in the gym; she made no mention of their ballhandling skills.[15]

Apple especially emphasizes the insistence with which the kindergarten distinguishes, and requires the children to distinguish, work from play, although they don't get paid for either. What I find most interesting about this process is the way the school adumbrates the fragmentation of labor in the modern industrial context and the corresponding neglect of, or contempt for, craftmanship as useless and irrelevant, and not only with respect to ballhandling:

> The point of work activities was to *do* them, not necessarily to do them well. By the second day of school, many children hastily finished their assigned tasks in order to join their friends playing with toys. During music, for example, the teacher exhorted the children to sing loudly. Neither tunefulness, rhythm, purity of tone nor mood were mentioned to the children or expected of them. It was their enthusiastic and lusty participation which was required. Similarily, the teacher accepted any child's art project on which sufficient time had been spent. The assigned tasks were compulsory and identical, and, in accepting all finished products, the teacher often accepted poor or shoddy work. The acceptance of such work nullified any notion of excellence as an evaluative category. Diligence, perserverance, obedience and participation were rewarded. These are characteristics of the children, not of their work. In this way, the notion of excellence was separated from that of successful or acceptable work and replaced by the criterion of adequate participation.[16]

This unconcern with the excellence of student performance has its counterpart in teachers' attitudes toward their own work, in the norms of the profession itself. Gerald Grace, in a masterful work called *Teachers, Ideology and Control,* discusses the evolution and development of the British urban public school as the means of civilizing and controlling the undersocialized—from the point of view of their middle-class neighbors and prospective employers—and unruly children obliged by the industrialization of Britain to dwell in unfamiliar and often squalid cities.[17] Recalling Charles Dickens' descriptions of the gradgrinding little private enterprises it replaced, one cannot deny the improvement. However, the verbatim accounts of dialogue between teachers and students in such articles as Viv Furlong's "Interaction Sets in the Classroom: Towards a Study of Pupil Knowledge," and Martyn Hammersley's "The Mobilization of Pupil Attention," certainly raise a question as to whether that improvement is as much in the intellectual as in the hygienic—mental and physical—level of the classroom.[18] In any case, Grace, in his study of how "good" teachers are defined by their administrative superordinates in ten British inner-city schools concludes that *"few teachers were selected for the quality of their pedagogic work as such and very few for introducing significant changes in either curriculum or evaluation procedure. . . . "* (p. 155); and *"In only a minority of the schools was the emphasis in typification of good teachers strongly upon the quality of classroom teaching or pedagogic skill as such. . . . "* (p. 167; italics in both cases Grace's). What is demanded and prized is something quite different, which Grace notes when the role of the urban teacher is first defined, and which has not changed much in function, though it has become somewhat less harsh in style:

In many ways the good teacher of the urban working class *epitomized a social and cultural antithesis to the imputed characteristics of the class among which she worked.* Against volatility and impulsiveness the good teacher counterposed steadiness and perseverance; against religious or political enthusiasms, an ideological blandness; against lawlessness and rebellion, an inspiration to respectablility; against native wit and unsocialized intelligence, an embodiment of disciplined study. The good teacher of the urban working class was, thus, seen to be the effective agent and countervailing influence against anarchy in all its forms.[19]

It is possible, of course, to argue—as most structural functionalists would—that even if all this is true, it does the schools no discredit. The lack of emphasis on excellence often is justified as a means of protecting children from feelings of inferiority and the experience of failure, at whatever cost to their opportunity to realize the potential they may actually have and to learn something more realistic about who they are in the world. At a more sophisticated, or at least sophistical, level one may argue against demanding excellence on ideological grounds, i.e., that the standards of excellence are themselves ideologically biased. This is not, however, altogether true. Ideological bias does, of course, affect standards of excellence, but it is relatively unimportant there if it can be prevented from decisively influencing decisions about what it is important to be excellent *at*. Basketball handling may or may not be preferable to streetfighting as an item to be included in the curriculum, hidden or revealed—and that *is* an ideological decision. But there is no real difficulty in developing and justifying performance standards in either activity, quite distinct from the relative value to be assigned to each. The same thing can be said of rock music and—but not versus—chamber music. Science fiction may or may not be a more important genre for young people to be taught to appreciate than the novel, but Ursula Le Guin, though pretty good, ain't no Doris Lessing. Generally speaking, this is a false issue, I think.

But a more fundamental and troublesome argument—the fundamental one for functionalism—is that, after all, the schools do prepare children to accept, function in, and sometimes flourish in the society that actually exists, which only the most romantic would deny is what they actually need. The schools are what society requires; they meet its demands and prepare their pupils to do so. I am not impressed by this. As Randall Collins succinctly observes in *The Credential Society:* "The 'system' does not 'need' or 'demand' a certain kind of performance; it 'needs' what it gets, because 'it' is nothing more than a slipshod way of talking about the way things happen to be at the time. How hard people work, and with what dexterity and cleverness, depends on how much other people can require them to do and on how much they can dominate other people."[20] It isn't as simple as that, to be sure—we do all possess a degree of free will and autonomy and, like Archimedes, could move the earth if we had a place to stand, though this is not why his principle is taught in high school. But against the full weight of hegemony, major alternatives are unlikely to present themselves as possibilities. Rebellion, itself, is channeled and molded by hegemony. The climax of Willis' *Learning to Labour* is provided by his insight that it is precisely the rebellious loyalty of the working class secondary school students who call themselves "the lads," their macho and anti-intellectualism that develop in angry reaction to the humiliations of schooling, that tie them most firmly in their place and fix them in their station in life.[21] Their employers require neither conformity nor affection of them, just a life-style and a set of attitudes that will keep them from escaping or tooling up their minds to raise the really threatening questions.

I had hoped, when I undertook to prepare this paper, to include within it some striking comparisons and contrasts between American and Canadian practice in schooling, and relate these to cultural differences, since authority and its symbols are generally far more salient in Canada and are accepted with better, if self-defeating, grace. But as I thought through this topic I came to realize that to expect this difference to be reflected in consistently more oppressive school practice would be to miss my central point; and, indeed, I know of no evidence that would support such a generalization.

Canadian schools don't have to be more oppressive, because Canada, itself, is so much more like a school. Members of Parliament are excluded from the Chamber and made, I suppose, to stand in the corridor for the day if they call another member a liar—even if the fact that he is one is highly germane to the point at issue. Aversion to any possible threat of disorder is so profound that it has so far frustrated any effort to entrench even a minimal Bill of Rights in the proposed Canadian Constitution; the provincial premiers have taken the federal government to court in an effort to block the process the Prime Minister has invoked, largely, though not solely, because he has refused to delete the very modest and conditional charter of rights it would provide.

Instead, if you live in Canada you settle for the tolerance and goodwill of authorities who accept traditional limits as a means of maintaining their authority but sometimes panic and throw their weight around, as when Trudeau invoked the War Measures Act and had nearly 400 people rounded up, none of whom was later charged with an offense, at four o'clock one October morning in 1970, under the clause that gave him power to suppress "apprehended insurrection." Nobody was shot or even beaten; it's just a question of showing who's in charge and not letting them get out of hand in the first place. Just like school, except you never graduate.

This is not, perhaps, the year in which to insist that American society is less authoritarian and more liberty-loving than Canadian—though I think it is. But it is certainly more anarchic and admits of more variety, which means that there are more ways of resisting it and more opportunities to do so. American youngsters are far less likely than Canadian—though perhaps no longer less likely than British—to internalize the commands of "that vast intellectual police force, set to watch over . . . their minds;" and many classrooms today resemble Matthew Arnold's darkling plain, swept by confused alarms of struggle and flight, where ignorant armies clash by night. Arnold's papa would not have permitted this sort of thing at Rugby. Far more develop a kind of armed truce between teacher and students, precisely as Willis and Furlong have described. Perhaps few teachers any longer think of themselves as wielding much authority, though they still feel as if they need it in order to do their job. And considering what their job is, and has been since mass schooling developed, they may be right.

FOOTNOTES

1. Paul Willis, *Learning to Labour* (Westmead, Farnborough, England, Saxon House, 1977) p. 66.

2. Willis, pp. 65-69.

3. Urie Bronfenbrenner, *Two Worlds of Childhood: U.S. and U.S.S.R.* (New York, Russell Sage Foundation, 1970).

4. John Eggleston, *The Sociology of the School Curriculum* (London, Routledge and Kegan Paul, 1977) p. 32.

5. Leonard L. Richards, *Gentlemen of Property and Standing: Anti-Abolition Mobs in Jacksonian America* (New York, Oxford University Press, 1971).

6. "Children as Objects of Fear and Loathing" (R. Freeman Butts Lecture, 1978), *Educational Studies*, Vol. 10, (1978), p. 74.

7. August B. Hollingshead, *Elmtown's Youth* (New York, John Wiley & Sons, 1949), p. 185.

8. Jules Henry, *Culture Against Man* (New York, Random House, 1963).

9. *Harvard Educational Review*, Vol. 40, pp. 411-451.

10. Ibid.

11. Ibid.

12. Ibid.

13. Ibid.

14. Ibid.

15. Michael W. Apple, *Ideology and Curriculum* (London, Routledge and Kegan Paul, 1979), Chapter 3.

16. Ibid. p. 56.

17. Gerald Grace, *Teachers, Ideology and Control* (London, Routledge and Kegan Paul, 1978).

18. Viv Furlong, "Interaction Sets in the Classroom: Towards a Study of Pupil Knowledge" and Martyn Hammersley, "The Mobilization of Pupil Attention," in *The Process of Schooling*, eds., Martyn Hammersley and Peter Woods (London, Routledge and Kegan Paul, 1976).

19. Grace, p. 122.

20. Randall Collins, *The Credential Society* (New York, Academic Press, 1979) p. 54.

21. Willis, Chap. 4.